Advance Praise for

"*God's Graffiti* brings the Scripture ⸻ ⸺ ⸻ stories or biblical 'at-risk' youth. In his powerful, practical, and inspiring style of writing, Romal Tune shows how God's love can and will reposition teens for greatness."
— **Phil Jackson, Author of *Hip Hop Church*, Pastor, The House Covenant Church, www.thahouse.org**

"In this book, Romal weaves his story in with the stories of some of the Bible's wildest holy heroes. He reminds us that our God is a master of the impossible, a champion of the oppressed, and a whole lot bigger than our mistakes."
— **Shane Claiborne, Author, Activist, Recovering Sinner, www.thesimpleway.org**

"The need for creative multigenerational ministry guidance and instruction in the church is great. Romal Tune has answered the call with one of the most creative and engaging texts published this year."
— **Dr. Otis Moss III, Author and Pastor, Trinity United Church of Christ**

"In *God's Graffiti,* young people can move beyond the media-fed illusions of perfection and myths of glamour and understand that God moves in the present, raw, reality of life."
— **David Ramos, Founder and Facilitator, Latino Leadership Circle**

"*God's Graffiti* will engage our youth with biblical ideas, personalities, and interpretations that will speak to their hearts."
— **Dr. Charles G. Adams, Pastor, Hartford Memorial Baptist Church, Detroit, MI**

"This book is inspiring and engaging! It combines the Bible and life in a way that renews our hope and our vision. I loved it."
—Dr. Joel C. Hunter, Senior Pastor,
Northland—A Church Distributed

"Using his own life story as the context, Tune demonstrates that no matter how much we've messed up or what others might think of us, God always loves us and remains with us."
—Daniel J. O'Connell, EdD, Principal,
Verbum Dei High School, Watts, CA

"Tune captures the essence of multigenerational, cross-cultural, and interpersonal life lessons grounded in rich biblical stories. I highly recommend the book for Bible studies, book clubs, and personal devotions for persons of all ages."
—Dr. Teresa L. Fry Brown, Professor of Homiletics,
Director of Black Church Studies,
Candler School of Theology, Emory University

"In *God's Graffiti*, Romal Tune doesn't shy away from the dark side of Scripture's most notorious characters, nor from the pressing challenges of urban life… and by doing so he puts skin on hope."
—Dwight J. Friesen, Associate Professor of Practical
Theology, The Seattle School of Theology & Psychology,
and Author, *Thy Kingdom Connected*

"In *God's Graffiti* Romal relates stories of the struggles of biblical characters to these faced by 'at-risk' young people in America. Having faced most of those struggles himself, he brings a very personal touch to what he writes."
—Tony Campolo, Professor Emeritus,
Eastern University

"Tune introduces an authentic and non-pietistic Christian faith response to real-life challenges facing marginalized in- and at-risk youth."

—Elna Boesak, South African Journalist,
Producer, and Human Rights Advocate

"If implemented, the strategies provided in *God's Graffiti: Inspiring Stories for Teens* will encourage, equip and empower not only this generation but generations yet unborn to fulfill their divine destiny."

—Honorable Judge David Young,
Circuit Court for Baltimore City,
Former Member of the
Juvenile Law Committee,
Baltimore, MD

"I recommend *God's Graffiti* to clergy, organizers and especially young people who need evidence that God can do anything but fail!"

—Michael McBride, Pastor, The Way Christian Center,
and Director, PICO Network—
Lifelines to Healing Campaign,
www.lifelinestohealing.org

"In *God's Graffiti*, Romal Tune offers timeless wisdom from Scripture and inspirational encouragement from his own life, which have the potential to change a teen's life forever."

—Margaret Feinberg,
www.margaretfeinberg.com,
Author of *Wonderstruck*

"From family dysfunction and temptations, to peer pressure and insecurities, Romal uses the Bible to encourage the young reader that they can conquer whatever adversities they may face."

—Richard Smallwood, Grammy Nominated
and Stellar Award Winning Gospel Artist

"God's Graffiti: Inspiring Stories for Teens is an oh-so-timely treasure with pages packed with wisdom and spiritual principles from the life stories of biblical figures such as Rahab, Moses, and Joseph. Most of all, as Tune depicts in his own life story, God's Graffiti provides divine evidence for young people to see that they can truly transform their life's tragedies into triumph. It should be required reading for today's teenager! Read it and reap!"

—Shawn Dove, Campaign Manager,
Open Society Foundations,
Campaign for Black Male Achievement

"With a moving, frank, honesty about his own life, and searing insight into the lives of biblical characters we thought we knew, Romal Tune takes us to a place of deeper understanding about renewal and redemption. God's Graffiti is essential reading; yes, because it is inspiring, but even more because in real and practical terms Romal Tune helps young readers navigate the road toward hope, and the overcoming triumph of God's love."

—Dr. Derrick Harkins,
Pastor Nineteenth Street Baptist Church
and Secretary of the Board for World Relief

God's Graffiti
Inspiring Stories for Teens

Romal J. Tune

JUDSON PRESS
PUBLISHERS SINCE 1824

Join our mailing list for updates and special offers.
www.judsonpress.com/mailing_list.cfm

God's Graffiti: Inspiring Stories for Teens
©2013 by Romal J. Tune
All rights reserved.

Cover design: Christy McFeman: Author Launch,
www.authorlaunch.com
Cover photo: Kawai Matthews, www.KawaiMatthews.com
Interior design: Wendy Ronga, www.hamptondesigngroup.com

Library of Congress Cataloging-in-Publication data
Tune, Romal J. God's graffiti: God's word written on your life/Romal J. Tune.—First edition
pages cm ISBN 978-0-8170-1733-0 (pbk.: alk. paper) 1. Men in the Bible—Biography—Juvenile literature. 2. Teenagers—Religious life—Juvenile literature. 3. Youth with social disabilities—Religious life—Juvenile literature. I. Title. BS574.5.T86 2013
248.8'3--dc23   2013004147

Printed in the U.S.A.
First Edition, 2013.

Contents

In memory of my mother,
Dorothy Molex,
1952–2006

Dedicated to my children,
Aman Tune and Jordan Tune.
You guys inspire me.
Everything I do is with the hope
that you will be as proud of me
as I am of you.

Special thanks to
Yolanda Caraway
Konyia Clark
Tina Flournoy
Penny Guyon, Firefly Media
Tashion Macon, Firefly Media
Rhoda McKinney-Jones
Lora-Ellen McKinney
Brian McLaren
Joi Orr
Larry Sampson
Delisa Saunders
Adrianne Sears
Doug Tanner

Introduction

I wrote *God's Graffiti* to make a point: Just like graffiti, our lives may not seem to communicate much of anything to other people. They may look at all of the problems, mistakes, pain, sadness, failure, or disappointments and not know what to make of it all.

It's the same with graffiti; some people look at it and don't get the message or meaning. They miss the beauty of the colors, the uniqueness of every line, the story behind the images, and the overall point that the artist is trying to make. Because we spend too much time worrying about what's wrong in our lives, we miss the beauty, meaning, and deeper story behind the experiences that God uses to write the stories of our lives.

Graffiti was once considered something that couldn't be understood, had no value, and needed to be painted over so that no one would know it existed. But graffiti (and its creators) has persevered and overcome the shallow opinions of its critics. Today graffiti is displayed in museums all over the world, and graffiti artists travel the globe to tell their stories, through this art form, which is a unique, complicated display of the artist's heart and thoughts.

All of us are *God's Graffiti*. At times our lives can be messy; our mistakes are often on display for people to judge and critique. Our pain becomes the focal point that distracts us from seeing the bigger picture. Sometimes when we look at our lives, they just look confusing, lacking meaning and needing to be covered up. But what we fail to realize is that through it all, there is a purpose, a direction, a story. If we stepped back and took the time to see what God is trying to say through the graffiti of our lives, we would see something beautiful.

God's Graffiti: Inspiring Stories for Teens takes a look at young men and women in the Bible who overcame family and community challenges in order to become the leaders we recognize today. Their stories and the ways that they overcame personal challenges give us some practical guidance for our own lives. You have the ability to do amazing things through your faith in God, the courage to try something different, and the help of a few committed people.

To understand why I wrote this book, you need to know my personal journey of faith through hard life experiences. I was raised in poverty, surrounded by drug dealers, gangs, and community violence. My mother was addicted to crack cocaine and alcohol. I rarely went to church and did not have strong spiritual beliefs for most of my teen years. I was the perfect negative stereotype of a young black man. But the truth is that no one wants to live "down" to stereotype. What we all want is the opportunity to be our best selves.

This book presents Bible characters and leaders whose lives were like those of many young people who are growing up just as I did. By showing the challenges that were faced by highly respected people in the Bible, the stories in this book can provide hope, guidance, and strategies that can help all of us to make different, better, and more spirit-led choices.

So, how did I come to make different, better, more spirit-led choices than those I might have made otherwise? It was not easy. It was a very long road. And it began by walking through the pain of being part of my loving, addicted, and sometimes violent family.

I must start by admitting that I have engaged in many behaviors of which I am not proud. I learned these behaviors in my neighborhood and from my family. I stopped them because of the devastation that I observed in my neighborhood and in the broken hearts and lives of my family and friends. I stopped engaging in them because somehow God's grace found and saved me when no one and nothing else could.

We Weren't Church-Goers

It took me a long time to find God's grace. My family did not take me to church to introduce me to God. Church is a big deal. Obviously, it is a place where God is worshiped. Church is also a place where a community of believers gathers to honor God together. Going to church represents a spiritual practice for people and their families. Church is a special and sacred space that is a routine part of the lives of many people.

Church was not a routine part of my young life. My family rarely went to church. There are only a few Saturday evenings that I can remember my mother saying to me, "Romal, tomorrow you're going to church." The next morning she would get me dressed up in a white dress shirt, clip-on tie, sweater vest, blue pants, and patent leather dress shoes. Once I was ready to go, I'd sit patiently, waiting to be picked up. When my mother's friend arrived with her family, I would head off to church. On those few occasions when I went to church, my mother did not go with me. I never understood why she didn't go to church with me. I wasn't sure if it was because she thought people in church would judge her, if she was ashamed, or if she felt it wasn't going to change anything. Regardless of the reason, I felt her absence strongly because I wanted us to be together and do things as a family.

In Baptist churches, you join the church (become a member) when you are old enough to understand the meaning of the faith. Although there were times when I wanted to join, I was too nervous and afraid when I was a child. The idea of being stared at by people as I walked down the long aisle toward the pastor made me nervous enough to second-guess myself.

There was also the issue of my mother. Even though she sent me to church with one of her friends, I worried that she would be angry if I made such an important decision without her permission. I was clearly looking for something spiritual to strengthen my life, but I remember going to church perhaps five times between the ages of nine and twenty-one. My family environment was filled with tragedy, unfortunate circumstances, and people making bad choices; religion was not part of the equation that was the math of my family life.

Instead, the equation of my family's life was a much sadder and less spiritual one. My mother was a single parent who was seventeen years old when I was born. Because she was so young and so alone, I spent most of my life with her family members: my three uncles, my aunt, and my grandparents. My relatives were loving people who stepped in and did the best they could to make sure that I was well taken care of.

My job was to survive and try to do well in school. That I should take school seriously was hard advice to listen to when they were not setting the example that school was important. We didn't have much money; my aunt and uncles held jobs most of the time but also had to find other ways to make ends meet. My family members were street smart and taught me about the financial benefits of selling drugs, the importance of respect on the streets, and the inevitable violence of the neighborhood.

My Family's Self-Sabotage

I remember watching a television show one day that told the story of a woman who had been addicted to drugs but was now in a rehabilitation program. She was getting close to being reunited with her young daughter, who had been taken away because of this woman's addiction. Two social workers showed up at the woman's house to see how much progress she had made and determine if they would allow her to reunite with her daughter.

In the show, everything looked fine, and the social workers were about to leave. But one stopped and began to check the trash. She found evidence that the woman had been getting high. The social workers told the mother that she would not be reunited with her daughter, and the poor woman screamed in agony.

I remember that one of the social workers asked the other, "Why did she do that? She was so close to getting her daughter back." And the other social worker replied, "It's called self-sabotage. It's when you want something so bad that you do something to mess it up." I'll never forget the day I saw that show. I said to myself, *That's my family*.

My uncles and aunt had lives that were examples of what happens when you engage in self-sabotage. They had great talents but were not able to get away from their personal demons, the challenges and temptations present in our community, and plain bad luck.

All of my uncles were talented athletes. My oldest uncle, who was a twin, had received a scholarship to play college football. His education and football career came to a halt when he went to jail because he shot and killed someone. His twin brother was also a football player who never pursued college because he was functionally illiterate even though he graduated from high school. For the most part, he hustled the best way he could and did maintenance work for people around their homes.

The youngest of my uncles was a high school baseball pitcher whose talents were celebrated in photos and newspapers. I often asked him to tell me stories about his baseball career and to show me his scrapbooks and photo albums. Coaches thought that my uncle was destined to play in the major leagues, but he did not pay enough attention to his increasingly sore elbow. He required surgery and was never able to pitch again. This uncle graduated from high school but never attended college.

All of my uncles were considered tough guys. Everyone in

the community knew our family name for the wrong reasons. The uncles who were twins had a reputation for violence. When I walked the streets at night or found myself in a dangerous situation, all I had to do was mention my uncles and people would leave me alone.

I never knew much about my aunt, a very tough woman who loved children. She always bought me and my cousin, one of the twins' daughter, toys and clothes for special occasions and holidays and took us on trips to parks, museums, and the local fair. In addition to caring for us, she took in her friend's son when her friend went to jail. My aunt didn't live the most legal life. She did construction work, but my memories of what she did for a living was sell drugs. She loved to knit; when she turned herself in or went to jail, she spent her spare time knitting the most beautiful sweaters for my cousin and me.

Most of the memories of my aunt and uncles are from times when we all gathered at my grandparents' home for the holidays. Typically those days would start out with lots of fun activities, great food, laughter, music, and stories about good times that we had shared. But most of our family gatherings ended with arguments and violent fights between the brothers or with their sister, who could hold her own. More often than not these altercations were the result of too many drugs and too much alcohol. Eventually family members would start leaving before anyone was seriously injured, and then the police would be called because someone pulled out a weapon.

Just as my mother was a not a religious person, so religion was never a large part of the lives of her brothers and sister. They would grumble and say that church was fake, the men who went were soft, church people gossiped, and preachers just wanted to take your money. The only time I remember seeing my uncles and aunt dressed for church was when they attended funerals. At those times they were not seeking relationships with God; they were going only to pay their respects to friends who had died.

For reasons that I never entirely understood, I was always curious about religion and would tell my uncles that I wanted to go to church to learn more about God. After they made it clear that they did not want to hear me mention God or religion one more time, I kept my interests in God, religion, and the state of my soul to myself. After all, these were people who loved me and cared for me. I wanted to please them. But I knew at a very young age that my family was unable to give me the spiritual guidance that I wanted.

Loving Me to Wholeness

I am certain that my family members probably considered how I would turn out a bit of a mystery. After all, my mother, her sister, and all of her brothers had serious substance abuse and legal problems, and they all were raised by my grandparents. Sometimes, time changes things. What I know is this: my grandparents were a blessing to me and were the main source of happiness and stability in my life. I firmly believe that the love and influence of my grandparents kept me from becoming a hardcore gang member.

My grandmother, Momma, was a homemaker who kept the house spotless and was an amazing cook. It's almost a stereotype, isn't it? I loved spending time at home with her.

Just hearing Momma laugh would make even the worst day brighter. If I was hanging out on the corner with friends and things got boring or dangerous for me, I would go to my grandparents' house. If Momma wasn't cleaning the house or cooking for the family, she could always be found sitting in her favorite chair—no one could sit in that chair but her—watching TV. She loved to watch cowboy movies and police and detective shows like *Chips*, *Kojak*, *Perry Mason*, and *Maverick*. I'd come in and sit on the couch next to her or sit beside her on the floor. I'd lay my head on her lap and we'd watch TV together. Most of the time I'd fall asleep right there on the floor.

As was the case with my aunt and uncles, Momma's personal story was filled with holes. She was not an educated woman and could not read. My grandmother was raised in Mississippi, but she never shared much information about her family with me. When one of my cousins began a family tree a few years ago, I was shocked to learn that my grandmother was previously married and had had another child. No one knows why she left, but it must have been pretty bad for her to leave her child. She met my grandfather when they were both working in a Civil Conservation Camp. These camps were part of a work relief program in the 1930s and '40s for poor people during the Great Depression. I guess that's where my grandparents fell in love. Later on Momma traveled with my grandfather to California, never returning to Mississippi. My grandmother had a heart of gold. She treated everyone she met with love and would help anyone she could, whether they were a neighbor or a relative. She gave that love to me; she seemed to know how much I needed it. Maybe she was determined that her love would make me turn out all right. Maybe she wanted to give me what her parents have never given her. I don't know. But Momma really loved me.

My grandmother was the first person I ever heard pray. Every night she would go to her bedroom. As I relaxed on the couch in the living room, I would hear her recapping the events of the day. After she talked about the needs of her children and the family, she would then ask God for help. My grandmother never went to church, but I know she loved God and strongly believed in the power of prayer.

When You Can't Go Home Again

My grandfather was a strong and hard-working man. He worked in the shipyard in San Francisco. He and Momma finally settled in Vallejo, California, where he bought my grandmother a small house in a neighborhood called Country Club Crest. Most people knew this neighborhood as The Crest or Killer Crest Side. There was nothing country club about it. It was a poor community plagued by all of the problems of any inner-city neighborhood. In this place, my grandfather, or "Daddy," as I called him, taught me a lot about hard work. This proud man worked at the shipyards for thirty-eight years without taking a sick day.

Daddy had his issues, though. He was an alcoholic. He drank every day, and he drank a lot, sometimes to the point of passing out. He and my grandmother argued about his drinking. They loved each other, but their relationship was not an intimate one. I never saw them hold hands or share a hug or any other form of affection. In spite of his problems, Daddy had a good heart. He loved my mom; she was his favorite child, and I was his favorite grandchild. It was great to hang out with my grandfather. I would sit in the shed with him while he drank. He taught me the importance of saving money, of working hard, and of having a steady job. Daddy opened my first bank account and showed me how to use a checkbook. Daddy even taught me how to sing the blues. Most importantly, he always told me he loved me. People in my family did not use those words often. The problem was that, like my mom, Daddy told me that he loved me only when he was drunk.

Like Momma, Daddy was a southerner, from Louisiana. He was unable to return to his hometown because of a terrible incident that happened when he took his young nephew to a store for beer and candy. They were standing behind the saloon in the areas designated for blacks to enter. A white man came to the back of the saloon for whatever reason and saw my grandfather holding a large amount of money. The man then said, "Where did you get all of that money, nigga, you must have stole it." Then he tried to snatch the money from my grandfather's hand. Daddy did not take insults lightly. He reached into his belt clip, grabbed his knife, and stabbed the man. When he fell to the ground, no one watching said a word. My grandfather started walking down the train tracks. His nephew asked, "Where are you going?" He replied, "I don't know," and that was the last day my grandfather's nephew or anyone else in my grandfather's family ever saw him. Daddy managed to get out of Louisiana without being thrown in jail or lynched. I imagine his actions were one of the reasons why he drank so much and why he sang the blues.

Daddy always encouraged me to do the right thing, and I tried hard not to disappoint him. He later developed asbestos poisoning from working in the shipyard. Seeing him with an oxygen tank and struggling for breath was hard. After completing high school I joined the army. When I completed basic training, I was blessed to see Daddy one more time before he died. I returned home in my uniform and participated in his funeral.

My Life as a Drug Dealer

Even though my grandparents did not have the closest relationship, it was clear that they depended on each other. I think in some way they had decided to become for each other the family they had had to leave. They were loyal to each other no matter what happened; nothing ever tore them away from each other. My grandmother always encouraged me to stay in school. Momma asked me not to hang out on the street corners with the other guys but, if I did, to be careful. She was the reason I stopped selling drugs.

When crack cocaine hit our neighborhood, everything changed. Everyone seemed to be selling crack, and those who weren't selling it were smoking it. It was the worst thing that ever happened to my neighborhood and to my family. All of my uncles and my mom smoked crack. I was never sure if my aunt was addicted to crack, but I knew that she sold it. After my mom became addicted, I had to fend for myself in order to eat, buy school clothes, and get everything else I needed. With so little family support, it was only a matter of time before I started selling crack. I never enjoyed selling drugs. I felt terrible for the families of addicts, and more than that, after hearing some of the terrible stories from my uncle about his time in prison for murder, I didn't want to end up in jail. But the reasons that my days as a drug dealer were brief had nothing to do with any of this.

One day after hanging on the corner selling drugs with friends I decided to take a break, go to Momma's house, and sort through my sales for the day. When I arrived at my grandmother's house, she was sitting in her chair watching TV. I sat down on the couch next to her, took out my money, and set it on the coffee table as a sign to her that I had money and I was okay. Then I took out the drugs and set them on the table to start figuring out how I'd move my last packages. As I sat there sorting through the drugs, my grandmother watched in silence. Finally she asked, "Romal, what is that?"

I said to her, "It's crack, Momma."

"Crack? What's that?"

"It's what they're smoking in the streets."

Momma held out her hand and said, "Let me see it." I handed her a rock, and she sat silently holding it in the palm of her hand, just staring. Her silence was deafening, and the look in her eyes saddened me. Finally she said, "Hmm, so this is what these niggas are killing themselves for, huh?" Then she leaned towards me, handed it back, and said, "Here." At that moment I realized what her silence was all about. Crack was killing her family. Crack and those who sold it were taking her children away from her. Crack had her daughter—my mother—living on the streets and missing in action for months at a time. I thought, *Yes, Momma, this is crack*. Our family had always had its problems, but crack is what killed it.

It pained me to reach out and take the drugs from her hand, but in that moment I also realized that I couldn't sell drugs anymore. I couldn't hurt my grandmother or contribute to the devastation of our family. I took the crack from her hand, gathered my money and the rest of my packages from the coffee table, and went back up on the block. When I got to the corner I saw my partner in crime—for his safety we'll call him D—the person who got me involved in the dope game. We had grown up together and were very close. If you didn't know him you'd think he was kind, but he had a short fuse. If D got angry, things got violent really fast. My partner was one my closest friends and protectors on the street. This is a guy who stood in front of me one night when someone pulled a gun on me and threatened to kill me. He was the kind of friend who would take a bullet for you if he had to. There aren't too many people who will do that.

When I got to the corner that day D was just completing a sale. I walked up, looked him in the eye, and said, "Man, I can't do it," then handed him my remaining packages. He knew me well enough to believe me. I even think he was glad that I wanted to stop. He was among the people who used to tell me I should go to school because I wasn't built for the streets, I cared too much. When I handed him the drugs he looked at me and said, "It's cool." I breathed a sigh of relief, turned, and walked back to Momma's house. When I got there, instead of sitting on the couch, I sat on the floor next to her and laid my head on her lap just the way I used to do when I was a little boy. Neither of us said a word, but Momma knew the important decision that I had made, and I knew she had saved my life.

No Choice but to Leave

Once I decided that I couldn't sell drugs or do any of the other things my crew was doing to make money, I had a decision to make. One day while my uncle and his wife went grocery shopping with the rest of the family, I decided to stay home. I didn't want to go because I was stressed over how I was going to get money. My mother was an addict, I gave up the dope game and everything that came with it, but I still needed money. School was going to be starting in a few weeks, and I needed new clothes. Normally I could have given a crackhead some dope to steal everything I needed, or I could buy it myself. But I was broke. When my family left for the store, I stayed home to come up with a plan for how I would rob someone. There was a nice neighborhood in walking distance. My plan was to go into that neighborhood after dark, catch someone walking alone, knock the person unconscious or shoot him (or her) if necessary. Then I would take whatever money he had and follow a route back to my neighborhood that would cover my tracks.

While I sat there on living room floor thinking through my plan, I realized that I didn't want to do it. There was the risk of getting caught, the fear of going to jail, and the guilt of knowing that I hurt someone or even killed for money. That realization led to fear and sadness. If I wasn't willing to sell drugs, rob people, or steal, then how would I ever make it in this neighborhood? My friends didn't go to school; they sold drugs, got high, or were gangbangers. If I didn't do any of that, I didn't have any friends. I realized that there was no way I could make it, and I needed to leave.

God Changes Everything

Research tells us that, for better or for worse, our families and their challenges and triumphs make us who we are. Our families are not perfect. We must accept our families for what they are, but we do not have to imitate the worst parts of them. We must love the members of our families as best we can and must always love the best in them. Neither of these things is easy to do.

This is what I knew about the challenges given me by the family I was born into: for most of my childhood, my mother was a drug addict and an alcoholic.

Two years after my mother became a drug addict and an alcoholic, I met my father. I decided that I wanted to go live with him in New Jersey. Most of my family, even my mother, didn't want me to leave California, although she was never around to care for me. Momma told me to move to New Jersey and not to look back. "There's nothing here but trouble," she said. I took her advice, returning only for my grandfather's funeral and a few years after that for Momma's.

When I left California to live in New Jersey with my father, I rarely heard from my mother. Almost every time I called to speak to my grandparents in California, they would tell me that they had not seen my mother for a month. When I did talk to my mother, she would make a lot of promises that she could not keep. It hurt so much to talk to her that I eventually decided to let go of any dreams I had for our relationship. I couldn't handle the emotional pain anymore.

All of us have pain, of course. And all of us manage our pain in different ways. My mother dealt with her pain by medicating herself with drugs. I was so heartbroken by what happened to her and by how our relationship was affected that there was no way that I would have taken drugs or become an alcoholic. I needed another way to soothe my hurts.

I chose God. I finally acted on my childhood curiosity about faith. When I was twenty-two years old, I was no longer as anxious as I had been when I was a child about walking down the church aisle to become a member of a community of believing Christians. I stepped onto the fast track to Christianity. I was baptized and became an active member of my local church; I accepted my call to ministry when I was twenty-seven years old.

At the time that God called me into the ministry, I hadn't talked to my mother in two years. That summer in 1998, two weeks before my initial sermon, I received a letter from my mother. It arrived in a long, thick envelope. I waited for days before I opened it, afraid to read what she had to say. From a lifetime of experiences with her, I knew that even at a distance her words had the power to harm me and to hold me back from being my best and most positive self. I made a decision designed to protect me against the possibility of hurt. I took the letter to church with me so that I would have the support of good friends when I read it. Following the worship service, I told a few friends who knew my story that I had received a letter from my mother. I asked them to sit with me. We sat on the pew directly in front of the altar. I did not know what to expect but, as it turned out, this letter was a wonderful surprise. My mother told me how much she loved me and talked about being proud that I had graduated from college and was doing so well. She told me that she had been drug-free for six months and was working to get her life together through a church drug rehabilitation program. The following were her exact words: "Son, I hear you about to become a preacher. I joined church and got baptized. I've attached a copy of my Bible study lesson with this letter and was hoping you would call and help me with it." My mother's letter blew me away. That this letter arrived two weeks before I was to preach my first sermon was the clearest sign from God that I had ever experienced. To show me the importance of my life's calling, God had returned my mother to me.

Everything I do in ministry focuses on how to help those who have been kids like me—kids who are hurting or who have carried the pain of their childhoods into their adult lives. They may be kids (or adults) who believe there is a God but are not sure that God has anything to say that is relevant to their challenging lives. Like me, many people seek answers to the question, "Is there anyone in the Bible like me?" or "Can great Bible leaders like Moses, David, and Esther relate to my experiences and my pain?" The answer is yes! These Bible leaders often led very hard lives, making them just like us. Their stories illustrate the ways that their painful experiences are much like those that many of us have experienced or are now going through. Most important is that many figures in the Bible became leaders by turning their challenges into victories. Because God changes everything, leadership and victory are in each of us. Turn the page, and I'll show you the path that God has laid out for you in the stories of each of these at-risk youth in the Bible. See how God takes what looks like a mess and transforms it into something amazing — something we'll call *God's Graffiti*.

1

Moses

Wandering toward Destiny

Ending: Moses was a great leader, lawgiver, and prophet who led his people to the Promised Land.
Beginning: Moses had issues with abandonment and anger.

When people talk about Moses, they tend to mention his role as a leader. They recall stories heard in their childhoods about how God used Moses to lead thousands of the Hebrew people out of slavery to Pharaoh and set them on the road to freedom. Moses had the courage to confront the rich and the powerful. His was not an easy journey, but it allowed future generations to be free, to live up to their God-given potential, and to enjoy the vision that God had for them.

Moses did not begin his life as a leader. Moses had a challenging childhood and made many mistakes when he was a young man that could have taken him down a far different path. But the mistakes Moses made early in his life didn't determine his future. Many of us think that the mistakes we

The failures of your past do not have to determine your future. make control who we are and govern what our lives will be when we are older.

Moses, like others in the Bible and persons in our current lives, provides lots of evidence that our mistakes, challenges, and life circumstances don't have to set limits on our potential. We all have opportunities to accept responsibility for our mistakes, deal with their consequences, and learn from those experiences in order to grow emotionally. None of us need to be permanently stuck in the neighborhoods, family problems, poor school systems, poverty, addictions, and other difficulties that may have been part of our childhoods. The failures of our pasts do not have to determine our futures. Like Moses, we can choose to go in a different direction, not allowing our fears or our pasts to haunt us. We can choose, instead, to live fully in God's purpose for our lives.

The Pain of Abandonment

At three months of age Moses was abandoned by his mother, Jochebed. It wasn't that she didn't love him; instead, Jochebed believed that letting Moses go was the only way to save his life. This had to be a difficult decision for her. The Bible says that in his mother's eyes, Moses was a fine child. You can imagine that like any mother, when she looked at him she imagined a future filled with great dreams. Jochebed probably thought about how talented Moses would become and the many things he would achieve in his life.

Jochebed was one of many Hebrews living in Egypt under the oppressive rule of the pharaoh. Because Pharaoh was terrified of losing his power, he made a decree (an order) that all infant Jewish boys were to be drowned in the Nile. To save her son's life, Jochebed first hid Moses for three months. During that time she must have watched Pharaoh's palace. Perhaps she noticed that the princess bathed in the river at the same time and place each day. Somehow she came up with a plan to save Moses' life. Jochebed placed Moses in a watertight wooden chest made of bulrushes, a kind of wetland plant, and pitch, special waterproofing mud. She set the chest afloat in the Nile River; Miriam, her daughter, watched over the floating chest from a distance to ensure that the princess found Moses.

It took a lot of courage and faith to do what Jochebed did to save her son. She protected the life and future of her child by giving him up. Surely she did not make that choice lightly, and it is easy to imagine how she grieved the loss of her baby boy. What other options did she have? Maybe she could have asked someone else to take her son and raise him, but she may have felt there was no one she could trust. Maybe she could have found someone in her family to take care of him, but it may have been the case that no one in her family was around. There may have been other options, perhaps better options, but for some reason Jochebed felt that the best that she could do was to safely place him in the Nile knowing that someone would find him. Letting Moses go was probably the greatest pain in her life and most difficult thing she ever had to do, but perhaps in her heart she believed he would be okay.

All parents must make difficult decisions. Parents must determine how many jobs they have to work in order to pay the bills and what kind of home they can afford. They must also decide whether they are too young to raise their children, too poor or unable to provide for and protect their children, or whether their children may have a better life if they are raised by someone else.

Every child who has experienced being raised by or cared for by someone other than his or her biological parents has questions about it. Many wish for nothing more than to tell their parents that all they want is to be loved by them. When we don't feel loved by our parents or have not had the chance to at least talk to them about why they left us, we can feel rejected.

People who feel hurt and rejected respond in two primary ways. One way is by internalizing our feelings. We turn our anger and resentment and grief inside out and learn to hate ourselves. We get depressed, eat too much or too little, and are moody or angry. Our bodies may also be affected—our stomachs get upset, our skin breaks out. The second way is by externalizing our feelings through destructive behaviors. We act out. We begin to get bad grades. We hang out with the wrong crowd. We deal with our pain by abusing over-the-counter medications, illegal drugs, or alcohol. We shut down.

We don't always realize that the things we are doing are a result of feelings we have held onto because of the anger, fear, and rejection we have experienced. The story of Jochebed and Moses makes it clear that some parents give their children up for the best of reasons. Some parents stay in our homes and create chaos. Other parents are ineffective. Whatever your story, God is available to you. God always has your back. And importantly, just as the Lord did for Moses, God makes other people available to you who can step in to aid you. Sometimes they make themselves obvious. Sometimes you have to look for them. Later in this chapter you will see that when Moses needed support God sent his brother, Aaron, to stand by his side so that he wouldn't feel alone and insecure (Exodus 4:13-16). God will never abandon you, but God will always send someone to help if you are open to receiving that person into your life.

Overcoming Abandonment

Some of us are a lot like Moses, with parents who weren't present when we were young—for a variety of reasons ranging from the protective to the neglectful. A lot of us grow up feeling we were abandoned as children. Our mothers or fathers were not there for us. They left or let us go or had someone else raise us. There are all kinds of reason why our parents aren't around. Some parents work two or three jobs and are never home. Some parents don't share custody. Some parents are in jail, are in and out of rehab, or go missing for months when they are getting high. As a result, there are young people who are raised by other family members or who grow up in foster care.

In my case, even though my mother was around, I still felt alone and abandoned. She was only seventeen years old when I was born, and like any teenager she didn't know how to be a parent. She still wanted to live like a teenager who didn't have a child. Most of the time she dropped me off with other family members or friends, who then took care of me.

A lot of children who grow up the way I did feel abandoned. Having parents who are barely there can feel worse than having no parents at all.

Though Jochebed made the choice to leave Moses where he could be found by Pharaoh's daughter, I imagine that it was hard for the young Moses to understand why his mother let him go. I'm sure he wanted to ask her, "Why did you put me in the Nile for another woman to find me and raise me?" or "Where was my father?" or "Why did neither of you fight for me and our family?" During his childhood, there were more questions that Moses never got to ask. The absence of these answers had an effect on his life. Perhaps this is why Moses became an angry young man. It may also be the reason why he cared for the Hebrew people so much. Even though Moses lived in Pharaoh's household, it seems likely that he felt like an outsider; knowing he was adopted, he seemed to identify first with other Hebrews as his family. Moses also knew what pain felt like. The politics of slavery had forced his mother to give him up. This would make anyone angry.

What Moses didn't know was that although his mother let him go, she had a plan for how to stay in his life even if from a distance. What Moses didn't know was that when Jochebed placed him in the Nile she knew the princess would find him, and when she did things worked out in such a way that Jochebed was able to take care of him for a while. For at least the first three years of his life, Moses had his biological mother close by (although he may have known her only as his nurse). Like many young women today, Jochebed made the best of a bad situation; she let go but continued to care for Moses to the extent that circumstances and safety allowed her to do so. Moses would have memories of his birth family because of the time his mother was able to care for him.

There are reasons why parents have to let their children go. Immaturity, incarceration, addiction, physical or mental health issues—all these are factors that compel parents to let go of their children, whether voluntarily or not. Most of us may never get the chance to question our parents about their decisions. And like Moses, unless our emotional pain is addressed, it will show up and we will act it out.

We overcome pain by confronting it. For years I was angry with my mother, but later I learned that she had done the best she could with what she knew. As Maya Angelou is credited with saying, "When you know better, you do better." As an adult I was given the opportunity to attend counseling with my mother; with the guidance of a therapist I felt safe enough to ask hard questions, to tell my mother how I felt, and to hear her side of the story. After hearing me speak, she said that she had never wanted the things she did to cause me so much pain. She expressed her love for me and said that she was sorry for everything that happened. That was a moment of freedom for both of us. For so many of us who have felt abandoned by parents or are confused about the way that they left our lives, the only thing we want to hear from them is, "I'm sorry," "I didn't know that I hurt you so much," and "I never wanted my actions to cause you pain."

I was fortunate enough to be in the safe space of a counselor's office and talk to my mother about how I felt. Not everyone will have the chance to work things out with their parents, but it is still possible to talk to a professional about

> The only thing we want to hear from the people who are supposed to love us is, "I'm sorry," "I didn't know that I hurt you so much," and "I never wanted my actions to cause you pain."

your feelings of loss, abandonment, anger, and fear.

The first step to healing and moving on from early emotional wounds is being honest with yourself: your experiences of parental abandonment and rejection probably affect your everyday life. Becoming whole also requires finding constructive ways to overcome your pain and find healing. There are any number of ways to do this that will be specific to your situation. You can pray to God about the ways you have been hurt, the people who have hurt you, and the help that you need to heal your unique heart. God will help you heal. Healing is a journey that begins when you are honest with yourself, honest with God, and honest with or about the people who have caused you pain.

Anger Can Get the Best of You

Moses' first childhood challenge was being strategically released from his mother's loving arms into the parenting of another woman and the care of her family. When Moses was a young man he was faced with another significant challenge. He was a Hebrew, and the Hebrews were slaves in Egypt. Moses was deeply concerned about how the Hebrew people were treated; he also had a terrible temper. One day his temper and his concern collided. The Bible tells us, "One day, after Moses had grown up, he went out to where his own people were and watched them at their hard labor. He saw an Egyptian beating a Hebrew, one of his own people. Looking this way and that and seeing no one, he killed the Egyptian and hid him in the sand" (Exodus 2:11-12). When he found out that someone saw him commit murder, Moses left town to escape the punishment that he would have received from Pharaoh.

According to the American Psychological Association, "anger is a natural, adaptive response to threats; it inspires powerful, often aggressive, feelings and behaviors, which allow us to fight and to defend ourselves when we are attacked. A certain amount of anger is necessary to our survival."[1] Anger also occurs when we are afraid or are trying to cover up feelings of sadness. Moses' anger was a result of the sadness he experienced when he watched the mistreatment of the Hebrews. It is likely that the enslavement of Hebrew people by the Egyptians made Moses think of his mother and the complicated reasons that forced her to let him go.

Sometimes the things that people say to us, do to us, or do to others are reminders of how we were mistreated in the past. If you were abandoned as a child, it might cause you to build an emotional wall to keep other people from getting too close to you, out of fear that they may leave you and cause you to experience the pain of abandonment again. If you were verbally abused by people in your family who made you feel like you were not valued, then you may feel threatened when someone uses words that make you feel as if you are not good enough. These words are a negative reminder of what you were told when you were growing up.

How we were treated in the past can affect the way we interact with people and how we respond to situations throughout our lives. Sometimes we have no awareness of how powerful certain people, environments, or interactions have been in our lives. But we can learn how past pain is still affecting us and why our emotions cause us to respond to certain situations. Most importantly, we can develop tools to help us deal with our emotional pain. We can find effective ways to keep pain and trauma from having enough power to get in the way of our goals and dreams. How does this happen? The first step is admitting that you have been hurt in the past, and the second step is admitting that you are angry about it. When you able to admit that you are angry and hurting, that puts you in position to identify the sources of your pain and anger. After you identify the sources, that information gives you the power to overcome the pain and anger.

One way to do this is through counseling. Another way is to find someone you can trust and tell him or her what you are going through and how it is hurting you or holding you back. Another way to deal with it is finding a support group so that you can be around people who have gone through similar pain and want to overcome it. Being around people who understand you because they come from a similar past allows you to support each other, to feel safe and understood. Most importantly, it gives you the freedom to talk about what you are feeling. Sometimes talking about what you have been through and how it has made you feel, with people who will listen and not judge you, empowers you to let it out and let it go.

I've always found that a good cry heals a lot of pain. Sometimes when we have been through so much pain and challenge we don't want to cry because we are afraid of being vulnerable and allowing ourselves to be hurt again. But I have found that it takes courage to cry. Anyone can hold in pain—a lot of people do—but sometime the tears become our source of healing. I believe that God uses them to wash the pain out of your body and away from your soul so that it no longer has the power to hurt you.

God Chose Moses in Spite of Everything

As a young man, Moses made some terrible choices; it's likely that his emotional issues about having been sent away by his mother played a role in his poor decision making. But making bad choices isn't a deal breaker for God. It does not keep God from choosing us!

The bad choices in your past don't stop God from choosing and using you in the present. However, Moses could not be chosen immediately. His uncontrolled anger caused him to commit murder. As a consequence Moses lived in hiding for a several years, running from community to community. While living in the land of Midian, Moses started a new life. He found work as a shepherd and married a woman named Zipporah, and they had a son. Moses named their son Gershom, "because," he said, "I've been an immigrant living in a foreign land" (Exodus 2:22 CEB; Gershom sounds like the Hebrew word for "immigrant").

> The bad choices in your past don't stop God from choosing and using you in the present.

11

Just because you move doesn't mean that you've moved on.

Even though Moses had left his past behind by running to Midian, he didn't move on emotionally. The mistakes of his past still had a great impact on his present circumstances. Moses had a new career, a new home, and a new family, but his past troubled him. His son's name was a reminder that Moses had become an immigrant, literally a stranger in a strange land. Moses had serious secrets; it was not safe to let people know who he was—a former prince of Egypt, born of Hebrew slaves, with another man's blood on his hands. Moses had moved, but he hadn't moved on. Just because you move doesn't mean that you've moved on.

Moving from place to place tends to keep us emotionally stuck. When I was a child, my mother and I moved from place to place almost every year. As a result, I attended a different school each year, from preschool until I was in the eleventh grade. I never developed close relationships with anyone because I always knew I would be moving. When I grew up, I continued the pattern. I was never comfortable in one place and was always starting over—from California to New Jersey, from Texas to Washington DC, Los Angeles, and a host of places in between. Some of the moves I made were necessary to pursue a great opportunity, but every time I moved I experienced the same personal problems. Each time something went wrong I would pack up and move to start over—only to make the same mistakes again. This should have been a clue that problems were emotional and spiritual; they had nothing to do with where I lived.

I've learned that if you move and still find yourself experiencing the same problems and same bad feelings about yourself, the problem is not the place. You can change your location, but your life won't be different until you make the decision to change *you*.

Do You Believe That You Can Be a Leader?

Here's the hard truth: Leaders aren't born. They don't always follow a well-designed path that prepares them for leadership. Leaders must have experiences that connect them to people, problems, and communities. This is why it is wonderful that none of us is a perfect person; we wouldn't be able to lead anyone anywhere.

You can change your location, but your life won't change until you change *you*.

We already know that Moses wasn't perfect. He had anger issues, and he apparently wrestled with a kind of identity crisis. But he also still had a real concern for other people. Even on the run, he was willing to stop and help out strangers in need. That's how he met his future in-laws. The Bible says:

> Now a priest of Midian had seven daughters, and they came to draw water and fill the troughs to water their father's flock. Some shepherds came along and drove them away, but Moses got up and came to their rescue and watered their flock. When the girls returned to Reuel their father, he asked them, "Why have you returned so early today?"

They answered, "An Egyptian rescued us from the shepherds. He even drew water for us and watered the flock." (Exodus 2:16-19)

That protective and compassionate spirit won Moses a bride and a place in his father-in-law's household. And it was undoubtedly something that God saw in Moses and would use to make him a great leader.

Life experiences can prepare you to be a leader. All of those experiences may not be positive. But what you learn from them can be put to good use. You see, while Moses was living a new life, his people, his Hebrew family (also called Israelites) were still living in slavery in Egypt. Because God cares for all people no matter what their situations, God needed a leader who would be a strong voice for the people against the Egyptians. Given Moses' past, you might not consider him to be one of God's top candidates for the job of leading the Israelites out of slavery. But God saw something in Moses and chose him to be a leader (Exodus 3:9-10).

> **Life experiences can prepare you to be a leader. All of those experiences may not be positive. But what you learn from them can be put to good use.**

God saw that Moses had the potential to be a leader, but Moses didn't have the same high opinion of himself. It wasn't that Moses didn't believe that God could do it; he didn't believe that God could do it through *him*. What was standing in Moses' way? Why didn't he believe that God could use him?

Moses had lots of questions for God, but none of them had to do with God's ability to help the Hebrew people (see his hang-ups in the next section). After all that Moses had been through in life, he still didn't believe in himself. Moses was insecure. He thought that God had overestimated his abilities. All of Moses' concerns had to do with what he thought of himself. He had self-esteem problems and worries about how others perceived him—and maybe he still had concerns about going to jail for murder when he returned to Egypt.

Moses' feelings were normal. It is human to wrestle with what we think of ourselves, our abilities, and what other people think of us. The good news is that God's response to us is much the same as God's response to Moses. For every human fear and insecurity we have, God has an answer that makes the most of our strengths and covers for our weaknesses.

The Power and Process of Change

Moses' conversation with God teaches us an important lesson: You must be honest with God about your concerns, fears, and insecurities. Moses shows us that you can tell God the truth, and God is God enough to handle it even when people can't.

Once we admit the truth to ourselves and to God, God can provide us with helpful and practical answers. As the Lord did with Moses, God created you for a great purpose. Our relationships and experiences can be the source of our personal hang-ups. We have to be careful not to let them hinder us from doing the great things that God has in store for us. Each of us has special gifts and talents. No one can do what you can do but you. Let's take a look at Moses' hang-ups

> **Moses shows us that you can tell God the truth, and God is God enough to handle it even when people can't.**

and how God responded. God started the conversation: "I am sending you to Pharaoh to bring my people the Israelites out of Egypt."

Hang-up: lack of confidence

Moses: "Who am I, that I should go to Pharaoh and bring the Israelites out of Egypt?" God: "I will be with you." (Exodus 3:10-11)

Hang-up: lack of trust in God

Moses: "Suppose I go to the Israelites and say to them, 'The God of your fathers has sent me to you,' and they ask me, 'What is his name?' Then what shall I tell them?" God: "I AM WHO I AM. This is what you are to say to the Israelites: 'I AM has sent me to you.'" (Exodus 3:13-14)

Hang-up: lack of faith

Moses: "What if they don't believe me or listen to me and say, 'The LORD did not appear to you'?" God: "If they do not believe you or pay attention to the first sign, they may believe the second." (Exodus 4:1,8)

Hang-up: shame

Moses: "I have never been eloquent, neither in the past nor since you have spoken to your servant. I am slow of speech and tongue." God: "Who gave human beings their mouths? Who makes them deaf or mute? Who gives them sight or makes them blind? Is it not I, the LORD? Now go; I will help you speak and will teach you what to say." (Exodus 4:10-11)

Hang-up: insecurity
Moses: "Pardon your servant, Lord. Please send someone else."
God: "What about your brother, Aaron the Levite? I know he can speak well. . . . You shall speak to him and put words in his mouth; I will help both of you speak and will teach you what to do. He will speak to the people for you, and it will be as if he were your mouth and as if you were God to him." (Exodus 4:13-16)

Finally getting it right
Moses: Then Moses went back to his father-in-law and said to him, "Let me go back to my own people in Egypt to see if any of them are still alive."
God: "Go back to Egypt, for all those who wanted to kill you are dead. . . . When you return to Egypt, see that you perform before Pharaoh all the wonders I have given you the power to do." (Exodus 4:18-19,21)

After all his questions had been asked and answered, Moses was able to trust that his faith in God had been well-placed. Moses knew that God would provide him with all of the tools that he would need to overcome his fears, his failures, and the ghosts of his past so that he could become the leader that was required to bring his community out of bondage in Egypt.

That is the lesson of Moses: You must also believe that God will be with you as you confront your past, explore your gifts, and live out your destiny. You may not know what you're going to say when you confront your past, but making the first step to go back is the hardest part. Be honest with God about how you feel, and ask the Holy Spirit to give you the words to say. If you don't believe that you can do it, ask God to give you the strength and confidence that you need to succeed. And remember this important rule of life with God: You are never alone.

Moses had to build up the courage to believe in himself and to trust God. The good news is that because God knew all of Moses' insecurities. God also knew that Moses would feel more confident if he didn't have to do this large task by himself. Sometimes we are afraid to lead or make changes in our lives because we don't want to do it by ourselves. Even before God spoke to Moses, God had already prepared Moses' brother, Aaron, to help him.

Theologian and author Jim Wallis tells us, "Faith is believing in spite of the evidence and watching the evidence change."

This is great news for us! God supports us in our leadership. God does not ask us to do it by ourselves. Not only does God's Spirit go with us on our leadership journeys, but also God sends reinforcements to sustain and encourage us. God wants us to know that every part of our lives—how we were or were not parented, our mistakes, our difficulties and challenges, our joys and triumphs—are all essential to who we are. Each of these pieces helps us become a leader.

> **Faith is believing in spite of the evidence and watching the evidence change.**
> **—Jim Wallis**

Sometimes the fear of failure is so high that it is easier not to try. We *must* remember one important fact: As our Creator, God knows what we can do and has given each of us specific skills and talents. We have to have the courage to try on our leadership caps knowing that there will always be at least one person willing to walk alongside us. Just like Moses, we have to take the first step and say to ourselves and God, "I am willing to try." Once you take the first step, start looking for that person God has been preparing to walk alongside you and encourage your role as a leader.

Beginning: Moses had issues with abandonment and anger.
Ending: Moses was a great leader, lawgiver, and prophet who led his people to the Promised Land.
What made the difference: Moses decided to confront the source of his hang-ups, his past. By trusting God and with the help of caring people, he was able to overcome the pain of his past and find his greater purpose. Now it's your turn.

What Now?

The following are activities that can be completed and questions that can be answered in Christian education classes or Bible study or written as answers in a journal that records your spiritual journey.

1. Moses had to overcome things that happened in his past because they had a negative impact on how he felt about himself and what he could do. What are some issues from your past that are having a negative impact on how you think about yourself?

2. What can you do to overcome those issues of the past so that you can finally move forward into your purpose?

3. Moses needed Aaron to support and encourage him along the journey. Who is your Aaron? Think of two people who have been there for you or who would be there for you if you asked. Write their names below and how they can help you.

   a.

   b.

4. Moses was honest with God about the doubts he had about his own abilities. What did you learn from the conversation that Moses had with God?

5. How can you apply this to your own life?

6. What are the conversations you have had with God about your insecurities?

7. In order to find your purpose you can't do it alone. When Moses needed help, God sent his brother, Aaron, to help him. Who in your life can walk alongside you and encourage you on the journey to fulfill your purpose?

Get Prayed Up

Dear Lord, I am willing to let go of fear and to throw out all of my excuses. Things that happened in the past have affected the way I feel about myself. But, God, I want to overcome those things that make me feel like I'm not good enough, and I need your help. Teach me to forgive myself for my mistakes; help me to accept your love and forgiveness. I know that I am not a mistake, and I know that my life has purpose. God, help me to feel like it, help me to believe it deep down inside. Lord, I need you, and I need someone to stand with me when I am weak. Please send me an Aaron who will help me to be strong, so that I am not alone. Use me to do things that will change my life and the lives of others so that we can be free to do your will and each of us fulfills our purpose. Amen.

Notes

1. "Controlling Anger before It Controls You," American Psychological Association, http://www.apa.org/topics/anger/control.aspx# (accessed April 12, 2011).

2

Rahab

What They Call You Doesn't Define You

Ending: Rahab assisted the Israelites in capturing the city of Jericho and saved her entire family.
Beginning: Rahab was called a prostitute.

Then Joshua son of Nun secretly sent two spies from Shittim. "Go look over the land," he said, "especially Jericho." So they went and entered the house of a prostitute named Rahab and stayed there. (Joshua 2:1 NIV)

Spy stories are always exciting. Their excitement comes from what we have seen in movies and on television; there are chases down dark alleys and into strange, dangerous territory. In this story, Rahab met two spies who were sent into her community by their leader to "look over the land" and return with a report on the people and their weaknesses.

In biblical times, as it is now, spying was a serious crime. But spying can also be an important way that information is shared in difficult times. Though Moses had led the people of God through the desert, he had died. Now their leader, Joshua, had to make certain that they were safe before they entered the promised land of Canaan. He sent two spies into Jericho, a fortified or protected city.

On the Jericho city wall there was an inn run by a woman named Rahab. She hid the men on the roof of her inn. When Jericho's king learned of the presence of these men, he insisted that she turn them over to his soldiers. Rahab lied to the soldiers about the spies' presence and said they were not at her inn; she risked her life to protect these men because she understood their mission:

> "I know that the LORD has given Israel this land. Everyone shakes with fear because of you. . . . Please promise me in the LORD's name that you will be as kind to my family as I have been to you. Do something to show that you won't let your people kill my father and mother and my brothers and sisters and their families." (Joshua 2:9,12-13 CEV)

The spies agreed to save Rahab and her family. They instructed her to hang a scarlet cord in her window so that the Israelites could easily locate and protect her family when they entered Jericho (Joshua 2). Rahab was a brave woman. However, Rahab was a woman whose name is never mentioned without stating that she was a prostitute, another way of saying she was paid for her sexual services. This typically is what we learn first about her.

Because of this fact, every time I read Rahab's story I get a little angry. It has always been a problem for me that, in spite of her commitment to God and the building of the nation of Israel, she is often more defined as Rahab the prostitute than as Rahab the courageous young woman. I've always wondered why she is defined by her behavior and not by her name or by what she did to help God's people achieve victory at Jericho. Was it really necessary to refer to Rahab as a prostitute? Why are we all so judgmental? This brave woman could have been identified only by her name, Rahab, and then the story could have continued.

However, the last time I looked at her story, God showed me something interesting. Perhaps pointing out her mistakes can show other young men and women that even though you've made mistakes and people label your behavior, God can still use you to do something great and courageous to help others, even members of your own family.

I take Rahab's story personally because my mother had her faults when it came to men. I hated seeing men mistreat her and use her for their own selfish reasons. It saddened me to see how men exploited her emotional vulnerability. My mother may have been addicted to drugs and alcohol for many years of her life, but that's not who she was. She was a compassionate and loving woman. Two of the proudest memories I have of her are the day I received her letter telling me that she had entered a church drug rehabilitation program. The other was when she told me that she was working with hospice patients—terminally ill people who had six months or less to live.[1] She was taking care of them, cooking for them, helping them around their houses, and spending time with them in their final days. My mother

25

would stay with patients until the day they died. What was extremely powerful and made me all the more proud of her courage and compassion was knowing that she continued to do this after learning of her own diagnosis of lung cancer and given only a year to live. Just as Rahab is always known as a prostitute, it was the case with my mother that people focused too much on her past and not enough on how she changed her life and the important things she did to help her family. Many people may remember my mother for being addicted to drugs and alcohol, but those people did not know her. They didn't have a clue about her kindness and concern for hurting people. How many of her critics would care for people who were dying, cleaning them, feeding them, and befriending them? How many of them could display such unselfish courage and compassion in the face of death after learning that they were going to lose their own life to cancer?

We need to stop defining people with convenient labels and to start knowing and valuing them for the whole of who they are. My mother was more than her addiction. Rahab was more than her profession. I think it's smart to stop defining people by their negative behavior and instead realize that there is always the opportunity for them to change and do something different with their lives. We don't know why people make the mistakes that they do or the pain in their lives that causes them to do things that are harmful to themselves or others. We should see their behavior as an outward sign of internal pain and figure out how we can help them turn their lives around rather than judge them or condemn them to a life of failure.

It's smart to stop defining people by their negative behavior and instead realize that there is always the opportunity for them to change.

By being the hero of the story, Rahab shattered all the preconceptions of who people thought she was or was capable of doing with her life. Thank God that other people and their labels didn't have the final word in her life, just as they don't have the final word in your life. Rahab became an ancestor of King David and therefore an ancestor of Jesus (Matthew 1:5)—all because she believed the stories about the Lord's mighty acts when even God's own people had doubts.

> It's smart to stop defining people by their negative behavior and instead realize that there is always the opportunity for them to change.

Knowing Is Half the Battle

I think it's safe to say that Rahab probably wouldn't have felt comfortable going to church (or the tabernacle, as it would have been then). However, it's clear that she believed in the presence and power of God. Look at what she had to say when the spies showed up: "I know that the LORD has given you this land. . . . For the LORD your God is God in heaven above and on the earth below" (Joshua 2:9,11).

Rahab didn't know God as intimately as did Joshua and the spies, but she knew something important about God: She knew what God had already done in their lives. She had heard about the amazing things God did to bring them out of bondage to Pharaoh and how God had given them victory against enemies in the wilderness. Even though she had not experienced God for herself as they had, the stories of the miracles that God had performed were enough to convince her that God was real and that those who trust in the Lord could count on God's help.

How about you? What kind of stories have you heard about God? Are you inclined to believe what you hear, or does it all sound like someone's crazy delusion or childish fairytale? When I first heard these stories, I thought they were fiction. I thought the people who claimed that God did something for them were crazy or making it up. Miracles didn't make sense to me back then because I had never seen a miracle with my own eyes. I needed proof. But the more I spent time around people of faith and heard them share examples of how faith in God made them better people, gave them something to live for, changed their lives, put them on the right track, headed them toward better futures, or healed sick family members, I started to get a little curious. Now I see a miracle every time I look in the mirror.

> **Miracles didn't make sense to me back then because I had never seen a miracle with my own eyes ...Now I see a miracle every time I look in the mirror.**

I wouldn't admit to being curious at first. I didn't want people to think they had the power to convince me of anything by their mere words. Where I came from, we called that ear hustling. Ear hustling was a good lie; someone used slick or smooth words to persuade you to do and believe what you otherwise wouldn't believe and do. To fall for this kind of con was a sign of weakness. That's why I didn't want anyone to think I started believing their stories about God. I didn't trust those who told them; I couldn't be sure if they were just like the ear hustlers I left in the hood. And I wasn't sure if they were trying to get something out of me. I didn't want them to think that I was weak or dumb enough to buy magical stories about how God had the power to change anything at all.

Now, don't misunderstand me. Many of the people I hung out with on the corners had active prayer lives, mostly asking God to protect them and their children from danger. (When you're living the street life, you pray a lot!) Just because people are on the street doing things that could cause them harm or keep them from living out their true purposes doesn't mean they don't believe in God. They *really* believe in God; the problem is that they don't trust God's people.

There are a lot of factors that keep young people out of church:

> 1. Fear of rejection by people in church because they are different;
> 2. Fear of being ridiculed or judged because of their mistakes;
> 3. Shame because of their family background;
> 4. Embarrassment because of the things they themselves have done.

Do any of those feelings or fears seem familiar to you?

Because of how I grew up, I didn't hear much about God. The people I spent most of my time with were not the kind of people who were likely to share stories about what God had done in their life or someone else's life. Back then, we lived around drug dealers, gang members, and people comfortable with street life. God was a private matter on the street. I didn't start hearing stories and testimonies about the power of God and faith until I joined the army.

By then, I was tired of having nowhere else to turn and having people disappoint me over and over again. Like most people—like you?—I wanted a better life, to be happy, to know that life was going to get better, to have a purpose, and to know why I am here on earth. I wanted to believe in God, and I wanted to know God personally. Whether I was willing to admit it or not, the testimonies that I heard finally had me convinced that God was real. I sincerely hoped that one day I could experience God for myself. I can tell you that since I began seeking and trusting God, the Lord has done amazing things in my life. This is what *God's Graffiti* is all about. It's about letting God take what looks messy or hard to understand and use all of it to make something beautiful, original, unique, and special.

You have to be ready for a miracle to recognize that it has taken hold in your life. In Rahab's case, she had been living on the edge of society—literally in the outer wall of the city—for so long that she knew no one was on her side *but* God. When she heard of the Israelite army approaching and when she heard rumors of their military victories elsewhere, she knew that her home, her livelihood, and probably her life and that of her family were in danger. Rather than being paralyzed by fear, Rahab saw an opportunity. Rahab was street smart. She knew that God was up to something, and she wanted to be blessed by it. So she protected the spies and sought their promise of protection for herself and her family. She chose to get on God's side rather than live a life of fear.

You can follow the same steps Rahab followed and start changing your life as well as the lives of the people you care about:

> 1. Welcome the "spies" for God who come into your life. Give them a place in your life (your heart).
> 2. Believe what you have heard about how God has made a difference in the lives of those who trust God's Word.
> 3. Confess and believe in your heart that you want God to be Lord of your life through faith in Jesus Christ.

It's that simple. The hardest part of learning to trust God is being honest enough with yourself to admit that you need God and courageous enough to not let anything or anyone keep you from seeking God. This is your life. It's your future. Let others live in fear and shut God out. This is your opportunity to do something different and to make a change that can bring you the peace, joy, and hope for the future that you have been waiting for forever.

Trusting God means admitting that you need God.

> **Trusting God means admitting that you need God.**

Don't Forget Your Family

"Now then please swear to me by the LORD that you will show kindness to my family, because I have shown kindness to you. Give me a sure sign that you will spare the lives of my father and mother, my brothers and sisters, and all who belong to them— and that you will save us from death."

"Our lives for your lives!" the men assured her. "If you don't tell what we are doing, we will treat you kindly and faithfully when the LORD gives us the land." (Joshua 2:12-14)

Family is complicated. Our family members are our first examples of how people act in the world. They are examples of how we should expect to be treated and in many ways set the standards for how we think we deserve to be treated by people outside of our families. Sometimes family members show us their worst sides. In some families, families like mine, kids receive a lot of negative messages.

I had lots of bad examples in my family about how to behave. I got really screwed-up messages about how I deserved to be treated and how I should think of myself. My uncles always cracked jokes about me and picked on me. In some odd way they thought they were making me tough enough to survive the streets. They even thought they were showing some warped form of affection. My mother used to yell at me a lot; when she was angry she called me stupid and said I would never amount to anything. Some families are full of criticism. They don't re- alize that the words they speak are shaping the image that kids have of themselves. You may know how this feels.

It was such a blessing that my grandparents knew how to speak loving and encouraging words. The Bible is right: "The tongue has the power of life and death" (Proverbs 18:21). My uncles, aunt, and mother spoke a lot of negative and deadly words to me. I believed every word they said. I have heard Dr. Phil say that one negative word can wipe out a million positive ones. But my grandparents' positive words had more power than that. They always spoke life into me. From them I heard that I was smart, that I could do better, and that I was going to be somebody special. I held onto these words during tough times.

Even now, when negative thoughts creep in, I call on my grandparents' messages. Their positive statements give me the fuel to keep going. In addition to the life-giving and motivational words spoken by my grandparents, I have the Bible. Over time I learned to believe what God says about me and reject the negative things I heard when my mother was drunk or high on drugs as lies, fiction, not based in reality or the truth of who God created me to be. When other people, even people in your family, say negative things about you, the Bible is full of messages about how God sees you.

Family fiction: They said I was a mistake.
God's fact: You are God's workmanship.
For you created my inmost being. . . .
I praise you because I am
fearfully and wonderfully made;
your works are wonderful. (Psalm 139:13-14)

Family fiction: They said that they hate me.
God's fact: You are deeply loved.
The LORD appeared to us in the past, saying:

"I have loved you with an everlasting love;
I have drawn you with unfailing kindness." (Jeremiah 31:3)

Family fiction: No one wants me.
God's fact: You are not rejected.
"I have chosen you and have not rejected you." (Isaiah 41:9)

Family fiction: They made me feel like I was nothing and didn't matter.
God's fact: You are precious in God's sight.
"You are precious and honored in my sight, and . . . I love you." (Isaiah 43:4)

Family fiction: I am alone, and no one cares.
God's fact: God is with you, and you are God's joy.
The LORD your God is with you,
the Mighty Warrior who saves.
He will take great delight in you;
in his love he will no longer rebuke you,
but will rejoice over you with singing." (Zephaniah 3:17)

Family fiction: They led me to believe that my life doesn't have purpose.
God's fact: You have a future.
"For I know the plans I have for you," declares the LORD, "plans to prosper you and not to harm you, plans to give you hope and a future. Then you will call upon me and come and pray to me, and I will listen to you. You will seek me and find me when you seek me with all your heart."(Jeremiah 29:11-13)
God's fact: You are forgiven.

When Jesus saw their faith, he said, "Friend, your sins are forgiven." (Luke 5:20)

This is what God wants you to know: what you did in the past can only continue to hurt you if you hold on to the pain. All of us make mistakes. Plenty of people want to remind us about our worst selves. But the good news is that what they say loses power when we identify and begin to live into our true purposes. Think about this: What were the names of the two spies Joshua sent to Jericho? We don't know. But even though she is negatively described at the beginning of her story, Rahab is a woman whose name echoes throughout history as someone who took a stand for her family and helped the people of God possess the land that they were promised.

Beginning: Rahab was called a prostitute.
Ending: Rahab assisted the Israelites in capturing the city of Jericho and saved her entire family.
What made the difference: Rahab saw the opportunity to change her life, and she took it. She realized that she deserved better and went after it. She took the risk to do something different that would bring her closer to her family and even save their lives. Now it's your turn.

What Now?

The following are activities that can be completed and questions that can be answered in Christian education classes or Bible study or written as answers in a journal that records your spiritual journey.

1. What similarities do you see between Rahab's life and yours?

2. What is the most important lesson that you have learned from Rahab's story?

3. People have called Rahab terrible names: "prostitute" (NRSV) or "harlot" (KJV). She had to change their perception about her.

a. What name or names have people called you?

b. What is the new belief that you want people to have of you?

c. What is the new name (doctor, teacher, scientist, police officer) that goes along with your new belief about yourself?

4. What is the worst thing that you ever believed about yourself?

a. How did you get past those negative beliefs?

b. In what ways do negative messages of the past affect you now?

5. What positive messages have you believed about yourself?

a. Who said these positive statements?

b. How does this support influence your emotions and behavior?

Get Prayed Up

Dear God, today this is my prayer: I have made some mistakes in the past, mistakes that have caused people to label me and call me all kinds of ugly things. But, God, I want to change. Give me a fresh start. Help me to remove the labels that I have placed on myself, that I'm not smart enough or good enough. Help me to remove the labels and live my life in new terms. God, there have been times when I have been embarrassed and ashamed like Rahab, but you gave her a second chance, and I'm asking you to give me a second chance. Send people into my life who will be a blessing and create opportunities for me to do something different. Give me the words to say when I meet them. God, I need your help to make the changes. Please give me courage each day to work on new behaviors, new plans, and a new and marvelous future. Thank you, Lord! I love you and thank you for loving me. I am living into my new name. Amen!

Notes
1. Hospice care is a model of medical care that focuses on relieving symptoms (called palliative care) and supporting patients with a life expectancy of six months or less.

3

Jephthah

From Family Shame to National Fame

Ending: Jephthah was a mighty warrior who fought for his people and conquered the Ammonites.
Beginning: Jephthah was disconnected from his family and community, shamed by his mother's past, and rejected by his father.

Jephthah was also one of these kids who had a rough start in life. His experiences as someone who learned a lot on the streets became a blessing and a curse.

Jephthah knew that his parents never married. He knew that his mother had an affair with his father, Gilead. Gilead was married and had other sons with his wife. The only thing that the Bible tells us about Jephthah's mother is that she was a prostitute (Judges 11:1). Can you imagine how Jephthah must have felt, knowing that people in his family and community used negative labels to define and degrade his mother? Since that's what people thought of his mother, they were not likely to think much of Jephthah either. Jephthah didn't choose to be born into that situation, yet he was treated like he should be ashamed of himself.

Children don't choose their parents, nor can they be responsible for their parents' behavior. Jephthah hadn't done anything wrong, but from the way that people treated him, it was clear that he was being punished for the circumstances of his birth and his mother's reputation. People in the neighborhood turned up their noses at Jephthah, treating him as if he weren't good enough to participate as a member of their community. A child born into Jephthah's situation wasn't expected to amount to much in life. As you probably know, people can be harsh, mean, unfair, and unforgiving. Thank God, these weren't the people who decided Jephthah's future. And they aren't the poeople who will have the final word on who you'll become in life. Only God decides.

Understanding How Jephthah Feels

As we have already established, lots of kids know what it's like to be Jephthah. They experience the sadness of growing up in difficult life circumstances. Perhaps they carry memories of watching a parent drink excessively or use drugs. Maybe they have seen men take sexual advantage of their mother. It hurts to see and know so much damaging information at a young age, but these young people are unlikely to say anything because they feel ashamed or are afraid of being rejected or ridiculed.

I know exactly what that feels like. My mother's abuse of alcohol and drugs was like background noise. I spent more nights than I care to remember going without food while my mother was out drinking. I'd stay awake late into the night until some man brought her home. I knew that she was going to be taken advantage of, and I was powerless to do anything about it. Her hanging out until all hours of the night and letting men get her drunk was an indication of how little my mother and the man each valued her. I watched her use drugs and remember the harsh things she would say to me even though I had done nothing wrong. All of this broke my heart. It took me a long time to understand that her words were the result of her personal pain.

I can relate to Jephthah's story. The things he heard people say about his mom and the things he saw her do probably made him a hard person—the type of person who doesn't show a lot of emotion because emotions have to be hidden in order to survive mentally and physically. Not only did Jephthah's experience make it hard for him to show emotion, but seeing how his mother allowed herself to be treated probably had a serious impact on how he treated women. Seeing how men treated his mother and what she allowed were his first examples of what men do and what women will allow. As you will see later in this chapter, Jephthah makes a tragic mistake in his personal life, and it was a mistake that would destroy his daughter's destiny. I can't help but wonder: If he had valued his mother more, would he have valued his daughter's life more and made a better choice?

There is a saying that comes in many variations of the following: "Hurt people only know how to hurt people." In many ways it's their way of crying out for help because the power to express their true emotions has been buried deep beneath the pain that they are trying to escape and medicate away with alcohol and drugs. Some people will never admit that they grew up that way because they want to be accepted in society.

You may not have a bad family situation like Jephthah's or even have faced challenges like I did in my family. There could be an entire range of happy or sad circumstances that you have been through. For example, you may have been or are still being bullied at school or another place away from home. Maybe others have noticed you because you are different from them in some way that they find difficult to understand.

But here is the good news! As part of the process of healing from the pains of your past, you will learn that there's nothing to be ashamed of. You're a survivor! More than that, as you continue to make the right decisions in life and figure out what is from God and what is not, you can go from surviving to succeeding. As you will see later in Jephthah's story, he made a tragic decision that affected someone he loved, his daughter. A lot of people don't make it to life's survival phases, but you did, and now it's time to thrive! And it is time to take on the mantle of leadership and show others how to mend their lives into success. Some people would probably say I shouldn't be so honest about the things I experienced as a child. Why not? I couldn't live in shame that wasn't mine. I forgave my mother for the danger she put me in. And I thanked God that both of us came through as well as we did.

> As part of the process of healing from the pains of your past, you will learn that there's nothing to be ashamed of. You're a survivor!

It is also possible that you have been embarrassed by the gifts of talents and skills that God has given you. You may have a talent that makes you stand apart from other people your age. If you are smart, can play a musical instrument, are an excellent athlete, can cook really well, are good at math, or sing, do so with confidence. God has blessed you. As Jephthah learned about his talent for organization and for protecting the people of Israel from their enemies, talents are tools that can be used for leadership (Judges 11:4-11). The lesson, then, is that we all need to know that a good life and leading others is about more than just surviving our pasts with all of their pain, shame, and embarrassments. Most importantly, life is about learning to succeed and enjoy the present because you are free from the pain of the past.

Moving from a fractured to a flourishing life is where we need to be to make meaningful and long-lasting changes. Traveling from embarrassment to embracing who we are is remarkably freeing.

> Life is about learning to succeed and enjoy the present because you are free from the pain of the past.

Jephthah's Healing Steps

Remember that Jephthah was rejected by his brothers and sent into exile because he was born out of wedlock? Gilead's sons told Jephthah that he would not receive an inheritance because he was the son of a "strange woman," a "prostitute," or a "harlot," depending on the Bible translation that you read. It is the pattern of many societies to reject such children; they are turned away from dysfunctional families and communities that choose not to provide them with support and love.

The important question is this: How did Jephthah change family and community rejection into leadership? The answer is simple. He did what so many other teens do; he found other people who understood his experiences. When Jephthah left the community where his family lived, he moved to Tob, a city east of Syria, and found new friends. These were likely young men who, like Jephthah, had experienced rejection from their families and community. They "gathered around him and followed him" (Judges 11:3).

Simply put, these young men were not valued by their communities. They would be considered troublemakers, street kids; I see them as gang members. When I read Jephthah's story, I feel that he joined a gang. They hung out in the wilderness, dangerous places, places other people were afraid of and didn't want to go. I imagine that they did whatever was necessary to survive. Today the wilderness would be the streets in communities where young people go when they are rejected by their families and communities.

There must have been something about Jephthah that caused other people to want to follow him. We are told that Jephthah was a born leader; people not only liked him but also respected him and were willing to follow his leadership. Jephthah had learned how to be a leader and warrior while living in the wilderness with his friends. Whether Jephthah's followers were adventurers or rebels, these were men who were fearless about moving into an unknown future with someone whose leadership they had learned to trust. While in Tob, Jephthah lived as a soldier of fortune who served as the captain of his team. This group was courageous; they were powerful warriors. Jephthah's courage as a warrior was soon rewarded. Jephthah's reputation as a brave and brilliant military man grew. When the Ammonites threatened a war against Israel, the elders of Gilead asked Jephthah to lead an army to fight them.

Today, some young people feel forced to leave home and join gangs; many gang members join for the same reasons that Jephthah left his family and community. Often, they need a group to belong to, a sense of safety and protection, and something that gives their lives meaning. Young people may also join gangs to feel cared for and powerful, as well as to gain respect and reproduce the family they didn't have. It's easy for teens to talk about what they are going through in gangs because everyone has a similar story of pain and rejection, so that none of them feel as if they are abnormal or don't fit in.

I was gang-affiliated when I was growing up. Being gang-affiliated is different from being in a gang. Gang members have to be jumped in, which means committing a crime or fighting a lot of gang members at one time. Being gang-affiliated means that you associate with and hang out with the gang. I was eleven years old when I was jumped in. I remember we were all together and the time came for the friend who vouched for me with the leaders to bring me in. Out of nowhere he started beating me until I fell to the ground; then he and two others continued to punch and kick me until the leader told them I had had enough. Once it was over, all of us hung out, but while we were together my side kept hurting so they sent me home. My mom was home asleep. I couldn't tell her what happened. I thought she would be angry or not even care. I went to my room and fell asleep. My side hurt for days, but I never told anyone, not even my uncles, what happened. (They figured out that something was different because I started dressing like the people in the gang and wearing a colored bandanna attached to my pants.)

Because I was only eleven, the gang wouldn't let me do much. I was the youngest in the crew, so, in most ways, I was more gang-affiliated than a true gang member who would be called on to do anything they needed. When you are gang-affiliated, the gang allows you to do things with them but does not fully accept you as a gang member; they also keep you from participating in certain conversations, meetings, or activities (usually activities that require violence, drugs, and sex) in order to protect you. But gangs do more than just get in trouble. Gang members have families, take vacations, attend college, and have jobs where the people they work with don't know they are in or affiliated with a gang.

Gangs teach a dysfunctional form of leadership, one that is often associated with negative and illegal activities in order to survive. This is why I feel that Jephthah was a gang leader in the wilderness. I'm sure they had to do whatever it took in order to be okay in the wilderness: cut deals, divide up turf, be violent when necessary to protect what was theirs. Nothing was free; everything came with a price or some form of negotiation. This may be why, when Jephthah went back to fight for the community he left behind, he felt it was even necessary to cut a deal with God. As you will see later, it was a terrible deal. God doesn't need our deals. There's nothing we can offer God that he needs from us other than loving God, trusting God, and doing things with our lives that please God. Anything that God does for you or me is because God loves us and desires good things for our lives because we are God's creation and God desires good things for us.

Young people involved in gangs also have dysfunctional families; they never learn the rules about how to behave, so it is no surprise that their leadership structure goes against social rules. Like Jephthah, I knew that I needed to find a different way to organize my life if I was going to survive and thrive. I had to find answers that would help me save my life.

> There's nothing we can offer God that he needs from us other than loving God, trusting God, and doing things with our lives that please God.

Finding Answers

Kids join gangs to find a sense of community and answers to their problems. They later learn that their new family is attached to lots of complications and problems, including fighting, the use of weapons, selling and/or using drugs, following inconsistent rules, obeying rules when they don't want to out of fear for their lives, and living with the strong possibility of going to jail for their behaviors and associations. They learn that gang life is far more stressful, lonely,

> If you want to have peace and live out your dreams, the only way you are going to do it is to deal with your feelings and to talk to the people who are important to you.

and dangerous than it's worth. At some point, young people realize that in the gang, they experience the feelings of loneliness, misunderstanding, and sadness they were trying to escape in their families.

Leadership begins with being honest with yourself and the people who are important to you. If you want to have peace and live out your dreams, the only way you are going to do it is to deal with your feelings and to talk to the people who are important to you. You must be courageous enough to be honest with members of your family about your feelings. You must also look for some kind of support that can help your get rid of your anger and fears. This will give you the best opportunity to become your best and most productive self. There are organizations in just about every city that have professionals whose job is to listen and to help you find ways to become the person you've always dreamed about becoming. There is always a way out of difficult situations. There is always someone who will help you find answers. You *can* live into God's plan for you.

Whenever I speak to young people and adults about growing up gang-affiliated, I am asked how I got out. Whenever I am asked about having a mother who abused drugs and alcohol, I am asked what it took for me to emotionally survive this challenging situation. While the process of survival is different for everyone, the first step is that you have to want to get out of the experience that is dangerous to your well-being. Making your life better and finding peace has to become your number one priority. It has to be more important than having fun, having material things that other people have, and making a lot of money.

Getting out doesn't mean running from your problems and moving to another place like Jephthah did. Remember what we learned from Moses: Getting out is not merely about changing your location, although sometimes that is necessary for your safety and sanity. More than anything, getting out means freeing your mind and emotions from the thoughts that can bring you down. It is essential that you try new behaviors, experiences, and feelings so that you can move forward in your life. You have to stop believing the lies that others have told you about yourself and that you have allowed yourself to believe are true. These statements are not true! God creates people who are good and who are capable of remarkable things. We all make take wrong turns and make bad choices. But our behavior and our souls are different. We can all be redeemed.

I know that moving from one home to another is not necessarily a successful way of changing your life. As a kid, my mother and I moved all the time, and I ended up hanging out with people just like the people I wanted to leave—new faces, new names, same behavior. I had the same experience because I had not changed the way I thought about my life and my behavior. When I finally made up my mind that I was

> **Getting out means freeing your mind and emotions from the thoughts that can bring you down.**

> **Leadership is a process. If you can't lead yourself into new behaviors, you can't do a good job of leading anyone else.**

going to change my attitude and lifestyle to fit my goals, my life changed. When I started believing in myself, I found new people who encouraged me and helped me make important choices for starting on a new path. Those baby steps were significant, but more work needed to be done in order to make the changes last a lifetime.

Leadership is also a process. For example, Jephthah had to forgive those in his community who hurt him in order to feel comfortable with their invitation to be their leader. Unless you make these personal changes first, you cannot be a successful leader. If you can't lead yourself into new behaviors, you can't do a good job of leading anyone else. Even though Jephthah did things to change his life and get on the right track, he made a tragic decision that led to the death of his daughter. In doing so, he showed that he had not fully overcome the issues of his past and had clearly misunderstood what it meant to please God. Making mistakes is a part of life, but we have to be careful that the mistakes we make don't put the lives of others in jeopardy. Some mistakes are irreversible, and that was the case with Jephthah and his daughter.

> And Jephthah made a vow to the LORD: "If you give the Ammonites into my hands, whatever comes out of the door of my house to meet me when I return in triumph from the Ammonites will be the LORD's, and I will sacrifice it as a burnt offering." Then Jephthah went over to fight the

Ammonites, and the LORD gave them into his hands. . . . When Jephthah returned to his home in Mizpah, who should come out to meet him but his daughter, dancing to the sound of timbrels! She was an only child. Except for her he had neither son nor daughter. . . . "My father," she replied, "you have given your word to the LORD. Do to me just as you promised, now that the LORD has avenged you of your enemies, the Ammonites." . . . After two months, she returned to her father, and he did to her as he had vowed. (Judges 11:30-32,34,36,39)

This story is sad on several levels and leaves me asking questions: Why did Jephthah feel it was necessary to make a deal with God? Why was he so careless with his faith? God had already given him multiple victories and was clearly present with him. Why did Jephthah believe it was necessary to take the life of his own daughter? Why do people hurt those they love in such tragic ways? When I think about what Jephthah did, I can't help but think about my own daughter. I would never harm her for any reason. Why did Jephthah feel that he had to go so far to please God? Did he really think such a sacrifice was pleasing to God? After Jephthah fulfilled his vow, the Bible is silent as to God's response. I think it is clear this was not something God wanted or asked for in order for Jephthah to win. God was not and is not pleased when we harm the lives and futures of children. Neither you nor I have to do anything that causes others harm in order to please God or even

Neither you nor I have to do anything that causes others harm in order to please God or even think for a moment that it's something God desires of us.

think for a moment that it's something God desires of us.

Murder is the ultimate tool to cancel dreams and purpose. I don't know of anyone in my life who has done something so tragic to his or her own child, but I do know people who have done things that destroy the futures of their children. When I was growing up, one of my uncles kicked his daughter out of the house when she was fifteen or sixteen years old. She did something that he believed disrespected him as a parent and dishonored his home: She stayed out overnight with her boyfriend, and when she returned home, my uncle told her to pack her things and go back to where she had been. He would not let her return to his home. I never understood why he felt that putting her out and leaving her to care for herself was the only solution. My cousin, his daughter, was very street smart, and so was the guy she was dating, so in a way as time passed she survived. I say "in a way" because being put out and having to navigate through life on her own, figuring things out and turning for help to everyone except for her father, had an impact.

But my cousin is doing okay today. She's not on drugs and doesn't commit crimes to make a living. Those could have been easy options given where we grew up. She has a job and at times struggles to make ends meet. Sometimes I wonder how much her life would have been different if her father made a better decision and chose another option rather than putting his teenage daughter out and forcing her to figure life out on her own. I can only imagine the impact it had on her self-esteem, her understanding of love, what it means to be family, her beliefs about her future, and the limits it placed on her dreams or opportunities she would pursue in life. Whether he would admit it or not, his decision would impact her destiny.

Unlike Jephthah, my uncle did not take his daughter's life, but like Jephthah, he made a decision that would change her life forever, a decision that would alter her destiny.

One of the other things I learned from this part of Jephthah's story is that he brought some of the things he learned on the streets—or should I say, in the wilderness—into his relationship with God. In the wilderness Jephthah probably had to cut deals in order to survive. It seems that for some reason he felt that he needed to do the same thing with God.

Yes, God can use *some* of the things we learn on the streets or during our wilderness experience as tools to help us create a better life. But there are some things that have to go. We can't negotiate with God. There is nothing we can offer God that is ever good enough to justify the blessings God desires to bring into our lives. God does things for us because God wants to. The service, kindness, and good that we do for others is not done because we want something from God, but it is an expression of how much we want to show our love for God by allowing the Lord to use us in service to others.

Finding Forgiveness

Forgiveness is a big part of Jephthah's story, and in many ways it is a big part of all our stories. Holding on to anger and hoping for revenge against the people who hurt you is like creating your own mental and emotional prison. I once read a quote on Twitter by Malachy McCourt that said, "Resentment is like taking poison and waiting for the other person to die." If you want to be free, you have to choose freedom; in order to become emotionally and mentally free, you have to forgive. The elders from Jephthah's community asked for forgiveness, and it was up to him to forgive. When he chose forgiveness, that's when he was able to move into his role as a leader. Forgiveness frees you up to think beyond the limits of the mental and emotional prison that once limited your thoughts. This is the true essence of forgiveness—the kind of forgiveness that God shows us every day and every time we make a mistake.

The issue of forgiveness is much different in the case of Jephthah and his daughter. She knew about his foolish deal with God and that she was to fall victim to his bad decision-making. But somehow she was gracious about not blaming him. She even took time to grieve what his mistake had cost her. "But grant me this one request," she said. "Give me two months to roam the hills and weep with my friends, because I will never marry" (Judges 11:37). She grieved her father's decision and what it meant for her, but notice that she didn't do it alone. She wept with her friends.

All of us need the support of others to overcome the pain in our lives. Friends and others who care about you can be a source of strength when you go through the process of grieving what others choices have caused in your life. Friends can help you heal. Going to counseling and working with a professional therapist can be a big help, too. After my mother died, I was angry with everyone, God, church, friends, and myself and my therapist helped me.

By the time I was twenty-eight years old, my mother had started to change her life for the better. She had joined a church with a substance abuse recovery program, and they were supporting her through the process of getting her life back on track. I started sending for her to come and spend holidays with my family and me. Over the next several years our relationship began to grow and heal until she was diagnosed with lung cancer at the age of fifty-three and given just about a year to live. We made the decision that she would move to the East Coast and live with me. I flew to California to help pack her things and meet with her doctor. After I spent time with her in the hospital discussing treatment, she died early the next morning.

I told my therapist that I didn't understand why God would do this to me. Why wouldn't God allow me to take her out of her neighborhood and poverty to finally experience a better life? I was angry because although I was blessed to get out and create a better life for myself, I never got to save her by taking her out of the challenges of the inner city. I was angry with myself and angry with God.

But in that moment my therapist, a seventy-year-old African American woman with a confident yet peaceful demeanor and the wisdom of an elder, looked at me and said, "Romal, are you familiar with the Middle Passage?" She said, "During the Middle Passage, there were times when the storms got so rough that women were cast overboard with their babies. These women knew they would not survive, but they would hold their babies above their heads so that someone else could take them. Even though these women wouldn't survive the journey, they did everything that they could to make sure their babies would be okay. Maybe that's what your mother did for you. She knew that she wouldn't make it, but she found peace in knowing that you would be okay, and before she passed, she got to see you make it to safe shores."

Although my faith was wavering at the time, I got through with the help of my faithful therapist and God's grace. God has opened doors for me to help others who are hurting from the loss of a loved one, fighting to overcome poverty, or dealing with a family member who is a substance abuser find healing and the strength to keep going. Not everyone's story ends the way my story did. In some situations the poor decisions of family members make such an impact that kids don't bounce back and overcome them. That's what happened to Jephthah's daughter. There would be no story of overcoming for her. One day, if you are fortunate, you will be blessed with a child if you have not been already. Your job and my job is not to repeat the mistakes of those who hurt us. Our job is to sacrifice for our children rather than offer our children as a sacrifice because of our mistakes and bad decisions.

One day in church I heard a sermon about forgiveness. I went home and wrote letters to my uncles and my mother telling them the ways that their behaviors had affected me and what behaviors I had engaged in as a result. I talked about the hurt and pain I felt, even though it had been years since those things had happened. Now, though, I was ready to let go and forgive family members because I loved them. I could not change my family, because it is impossible to change anyone else. All you can do is let the people you love know your true feelings. This sermon about forgiveness had come at just the right time. I wanted to be freed of the painful memories, disappointment, and sadness that I associated with my childhood. I could do this only if I was truthful about those long-ago feelings, experiences, and perceptions and confronted the family members who had hurt me. It was important that I tell family members that I was ready to move on, and forgive them and myself. That's how you get out! Once you have freed yourself from your pain, the past does not have the power to hurt you anymore. As God is my witness, the Lord will give you the strength to confront your emotional demons and those who have hurt you. You'll be amazed at the changes in your life. You will feel confident about yourself and your future.

Several years after I wrote those letters I accepted a call to the ministry to preach. I shared with you previously that two weeks before my first sermon, I got a letter from my mother. It's important that I share part of that story with you again now because I can't emphasize enough the power of forgiveness, God's ability to heal relationships, and the courage it takes to do something drastic that changes your life or can even save your life.

After I read that letter, my relationship with my mother got better and better. I would send for her to come and spend holidays with my wife, my children, and me. She loved spending time with her grandkids. When she died of lung cancer six years later, it was devastating to lose her, but when I look at the courage and strength that God gave both of us to do the work of healing, I am grateful.

God wants the same thing for you because you deserve it. You can replace the pain of the past with peace in the present. It takes work, but it's worth it. And trust me when I say that it will change your life.

Turning a Bad Start (and a Mistaken Middle) into a Strong Finish

Sometimes what looks like a bad start will position you for a strong finish. When the Ammonites threatened war against Israel, the elders of Jephthah's hometown of Gilead sought out Jephthah. They had heard that Jephthah was a great military leader who surrounded himself with a group of exceptional warriors. When the elders found Jephthah, they asked him to be their leader and help them keep their families and community safe. But Jephthah had not forgotten how he had been treated when he was younger. He reminded them of his concerns, saying, "Didn't you hate me and drive me from my father's house? Why do you come to me now, when you're in trouble?" (Judges 11:7). The elders did not take responsibility for their past behaviors, but Jephthah let them know that he hadn't forgotten. Jephthah made it clear that he had to be given

> You can replace the pain of the past with peace in the present. It takes work, but it's worth it and will change your life.

permission to fight the war as he saw fit; he did not want to be tricked by people who had previously disappointed him.

> **Sometimes what looks like a bad start can put you in the right position for a strong finish.**

Sometimes people try to restore broken relationships without dealing with what took place to cause the break. That is not real healing; it's an attempt to ignore the problem as if it will just go away. I don't believe the saying "time heals all wounds" because it takes a second to burn your hand but the scar can last a lifetime. We have to deal with what scarred us.

Rather than going along with the elders and ignoring what had happened, Jephthah spoke to them about how their behaviors had hurt him. After all, they had judged him because of the circumstances of his birth. The elders (and his brothers) believed that a child who was a bastard born to a prostitute would not amount to anything good. Yet, look at him! He was a military hero who had achieved so much that they had asked for his help.

Sometimes we "go along to get along," but it doesn't last for long! Sooner or later our difficult pasts will challenge our present happiness if they aren't dealt with and resolved. The second time that Jephthah spoke to the elders about how he had been treated, they agreed that they had been wrong in their treatment of Jephthah and asked him to come home and be their leader. "The elders of Gilead said to him, 'Nevertheless, we are turning to you now; come with us to fight the Ammonites, and you will be our head over all who live in Gilead'" (Judges 11:8). It is an act of courage to admit that you are

> **Sometimes we "go along to get along," but it doesn't last for long!**

wrong. It is also courageous to accept an apology gracefully. The reality is that Jephthah needed the elders just as much as they needed his forgiveness. This process was good for everyone's souls.

Our families and communities are stronger when we stick together and fight for each other instead of with each other. People who have been hurt and are trying to move on want nothing more than for their families to come looking for them and work together to heal. Whether we know it or not, all of us want to hear someone say, "We need you, and we're not strong without you." We all want to be respected and valued. We all want to know that someone is willing to fight for us and not let us go once we have returned to the fold.

If you have hurt someone in your family, be certain that you have not created a protective hardened shell around you and your emotions. None of us wants to admit that we are wrong. Perhaps an armor of pride disguised as anger has kept you from restoring a relationship with the person you hurt. Well, go to him or her now! That person has been waiting for you to show up. Don't wait on the other person to take the first step. You caused the problem, so you start the healing. Deal with the drama. That way you can live without guilt in the present. Fight for your emotional freedom by asking for forgiveness.

Being forgiven is a difficult and painful process. Forgiving so that you can heal takes trust, and trusting people who have hurt you also takes courage. When the elders asked

Jephthah to fight for them and be their leader, at first Jephthah didn't want to trust them. "Jephthah answered, 'Suppose you take me back to fight the Ammonites and the LORD gives them to me—will I really be your head?'" (Judges 11:9). It is clear that Jephthah was worried that the elders might hurt him again. Rebuilding trust is hard work, and it takes time. Trust is more about actions than it is about words. You earn trust by what you do. Jephthah had doubts because of how he had been treated. He had no control over his birth. But the elders said something that made Jephthah feel safe enough to take the risk, to go back home and help his family during their time of need. "The elders of Gilead replied, 'The LORD is our witness; we will certainly do as you say'" (Judges 11:10). When people work to mend their broken relationships, God is pleased. In order for healing to take place, both sides of the conflict have to trust God to be with them as they work through the rough spots.

> People who have been hurt...want to hear someone say, "We need you, and we're not strong without you."

After Jephthah returned to Gilead with the elders, they kept their promise to make him their chief warrior and leader. Together with the community that had once rejected him and with God's guidance, Jephthah and his band of warriors defeated their enemies. "Then Jephthah went over to fight the Ammonites, and the LORD gave them into his hands" (Judges 11:32).

When we are able to say what we feel without fear of rejection, we receive validation and respect. That's when

> **Trust is more about actions than it is about words. You earn trust by what you do.**

our relationships become strongest. When we know that we are supported, valued, and are a part of a community that cares, there is no challenge that we cannot overcome together, because God is with us. How can we lose?

Are there people in your family to whom you wish you were closer? If so, you understand that repairing one relationship strengthens the entire family. You don't want to waste one precious moment. Life is short, and relationships are the most important gift that God gives us. Recall how wonderful it was for me to have a new relationship with my mother and to have her be part of my adult family and make her (and all of us) incredibly happy before her death. In Jephthah's case, strengthening his relationship with the elders also strengthened his community and made them safe.

So you know what to do. Start the process of healing by taking the first step toward having an honest conversation with your family members; it will start the hard work of developing trust. Keep your word, and behave in ways that indicate that you mean what you say and that you're willing to earn your family's trust. Talk, as they say, is cheap. Behavior is what is important. When everyone does their part to restore the broken relationship and heal past wounds, God will give you victories that you never imagined were possible!

Beginning: Jephthah was disconnected from his family and community, shamed by his mother's past, and rejected by his father.

Ending: Jephthah was a mighty warrior who fought for his people and conquered the Ammonites.

What made the difference: Jephthah had to learn the power of forgiveness in order to become a leader. In the end he still made a tragic mistake with his daughter's life. That tragedy teaches us that sometimes even good intentions to please God can be misguided. God gave Jephthah the victory because God wanted to and not because of any deal Jephthah thought he could make with God that would cause God to help him. In our efforts to please God it's more about giving of ourselves to help others rather than to harm them.

> God will give you victories that you never imagined were possible!

What Now?

The following are activities that can be completed and questions that can be answered in Christian education classes or Bible study or written as answers in a journal that records your spiritual journey.

1. What similarities do you see between Jepthah's life and yours? What are some of the things Jephthah was willing to do to change his life that you can use to change yours?

2. What are your three strongest leadership qualities? How is God asking you to use them?

3. Although Jephthah was able to forgive those who hurt him and become a successful leader of the people, he failed at leading in his home. His unnecessary bargain with God cost his daughter her life. What does his story teach you about why it is not necessary to bargain with God?

4. What are some things that you can do to avoid hurting the people you care about and not cause them to become victims of your decisions or your personal pain?

5. Have you made choices in your life that have done what might be considered irreversible damage to another person? Is it possible for you to forgive yourself, ask that person for forgiveness, and ask God to forgive you? How do you think that you should go about it?

Get Prayed Up

Dear God, I know that you have chosen me to lead, just as you chose Jephthah. Help me to heal from the things that happened in my childhood. God, I have been angry with the people who rejected me, mistreated me, and threw me away, and I need your help to forgive them. Teach me not to be ashamed by my past; give me the wisdom to keep my past from blocking my present or hurting those around me. Some of the things I've seen as a young person have influenced my behavior and how I treat people. I now know that the way I treat them is wrong. God, I need your help to change. Please send new people into my life to teach me new things and show me how men and women deserve to be treated with respect. I thank you, God, for guiding me every step of the way. Amen.

4

Ishmael

It's Not Your Fault!

Ending: Ishmael became the father of a nation.
Beginning: Ishmael was the disregarded son of a slave.

Here is the cheat-sheet version of Ishmael's story: Ishmael and Isaac were half-brothers who were Abraham's sons. Sarah, Abraham's wife, could not have children. She encouraged Abraham to sleep with her Egyptian maidservant, Hagar. Hagar then gave birth to Ishmael.[1]

> But Sarah saw that the son whom Hagar the Egyptian had born to Abraham was mocking (insulting), and she said to Abraham, "Get rid of that slave woman and her son, for that slave woman's son will never share in the inheritance with my son Isaac." The matter distressed Abraham greatly because it concerned his son. But God said to him, "Do not be so distressed about the boy and your maidservant.

Listen to whatever Sarah tells you, because it is through Isaac that your offspring will be reckoned.[2] I will make the son of the slave into a nation also, because he is your offspring" (Genesis 21:9-12).

Sarah convinced Abraham to banish Hagar and Ishmael to the wilderness so that her son, Isaac, could become the next patriarch[3] or head of the family. Ishmael and Hagar wandered in the desert for a while, but God made certain that they made it to safety. In spite of a rocky start, things turned out well for Ishmael. Through Ishmael, a nation would be born.

> We need not be ashamed. We can claim our names. Not everything that is bad is our fault. What is bad need not be our fortunes.

Each time I read Ishmael's story I am struck by how unfair his life was. The story of Ishmael is complicated, but it is not uncommon. His family life contains many factors that created challenges for him in ways that may also be relevant to you. Some of the details may be different, but the feelings and the outcomes may be the same.

Ishmael experienced family drama, and a lot of teens grow up in situations similar to his. These are complications that make it hard to understand who you are and what gives your life meaning. It can make it difficult to build self-confidence. Sometimes this is the challenge of growing up in a single-parent home, not knowing your father and with a mother who has to spend most of her time making sure that she and her child are okay. Hard times make many parents work more than one job just to make one salary. While all of us are products of our environments, we can learn lessons from our hard times and triumph over them. The craziness of our environments never needs to define us, even though it may have helped to shape who we are. We don't have to be ashamed. We

> We don't have to be ashamed. We can be proud of who we are.

can be proud of who we are. We can claim our own mistakes and missteps. But here is the truth: What has been bad in our lives doesn't have to lead to a bad fortune.

The Art of War?

One of the most famous lines in literature is this: "Call me Ishmael." It is the first line of Herman Melville's novel *Moby-Dick, or, The Whale* (1851). This is the story about the adventures of a wandering sailor, Ishmael, on a whaling ship called the *Pequod*, under the direction of Captain Ahab. Ishmael soon learns that Ahab's sole purpose is to capture Moby-Dick, the whale that had previously destroyed his boat and bitten off his leg. This was a voyage of revenge, not a great escapade.

As the story of *Moby-Dick* progresses, we learn a lot about Ishmael, the wandering sailor. What we also see is that he has serious identity problems. This trip was supposed to help him determine what he wanted to do with his life.

So what does all of this have to do with you? It's easy to spend your life angry with the people who hurt you, blaming others for why life is so hard or, even worse, spending your life seeking revenge or trying to punish those who hurt you.

> **Anger and revenge are distractions that take you in directions that will never make you feel better about yourself.**

All of these things get in the way of finding your true purpose in life, fulfilling your dreams, and living a life that gives you peace, happiness, and health. Anger and revenge are distractions that take you in directions that will never make you feel better about yourself. They only cause you to hold on to the pain and think that if you get revenge you will feel better. The reality is that you will not feel better. The only thing that will make you feel better about yourself is finding a way to forgive others, forgive yourself, and overcome the pain.

In *The Art of War*, Sun Tzu said, "If you know your enemy and know yourself, you need not fear the result of a hundred battles. If you know yourself but not your enemy, for every victory gained you will also know defeat. If you know neither the enemy or yourself, you will succumb to every battle."[4] While he was talking specifically about war, much of his advice translates to other aspects of life. An inability to understand ourselves leads us to make terrible decisions.

When you don't understand who you are, you question your talents and are not sure of your purpose or what you want to do with your life. This will make you fear the future. Experiences that make you feel you're not good enough and people who made you feel you're not good enough can lead to low self-esteem. Low self-esteem causes you to believe that you can't do things and that other people are better than you. When some people feel like this, they find negative ways to make themselves feel better and other people feel worse. They become bullies, they say negative things about people, they gossip and judge people. The reality is that when people treat others this way, there is nothing wrong with the other person; it's a sign that the people causing harm have low self-esteem. People who feel good about themselves don't behave like this. There are a lot of causes for low self-esteem and signs that someone doesn't feel good about him or herself. Here are a few causes and symptoms for low self-esteem.

Causes
Abuse
Abuse is too frequent an occurrence for adolescents. It occurs in many forms, as many of you may know. Most children and teens who are abused are neglected, materially or emotionally, by their caregivers. Others are physically or sexually abused. Some experience a combination of types of abuse.[5]

Divorce
When a parent experiences the pain of divorce, you will experience pain too. Divorce causes teenagers to be insecure and vulnerable. Teens living in families that have experienced divorce often become depressed.

Bullying
Experts estimate that half of all children and teens are bullied during their school years, 10 percent of those on a regular basis. Bullying can be physical or verbal,[6] and cyber-bullying uses technology (e.g., social media, cell phones) to harass other people. The incidence of cyber-bullying is increasing.

Symptoms

Drugs and Alcohol

Many teens experiment with drugs and alcohol. Drug and alcohol abuse are more likely to become problems or to lead to addiction when there is a dysfunctional family structure.[7]

Eating Disorders

Eating disorders are defined as the extreme emotions, attitudes, and behaviors surrounding eating, weight, body image, and food intake. Eating disorders such as anorexia (refusing to maintain healthy body weight) and bulimia (binge eating and then purging through vomiting or laxative use) can kill you.[8]

Sex

In every generation, teenagers have had sexual intercourse earlier than their parents would have liked. You may have already begun sexual relationships, but it's likely that you are not prepared to manage the emotional or physical consequences of such relationships, including the risk of pregnancy or AIDS and other sexually transmitted diseases (STDs).

Suicide

Suicide, the taking of one's own life, is a leading cause of death for children and teens. Teens kill themselves for a variety of reasons, including parental divorce, family violence, educational failure, social rejection by peers, bullying, substance abuse, and grief over another's death.[9]

Ishmael's Burden

As I mentioned earlier, Ishmael did not ask to be born into a complicated situation. Being born into a family where your father and mother are not together because your father is married to another woman is confusing for any child. Most parents don't take responsibility for their actions and tell their children what happened so that the child can try to make some sense out of the confusion and questions swirling around in his or her head. As young people we often try to make some sense of it on our own, which is hard because we don't have enough information.

Ishmael's story inspires hard questions —with no easy answers. What was it like to be Ishmael? Did he understand how his life was going to change after his brother was born? Did Ishmael ask difficult questions such as, Why did my father let his wife convince him to kick me out? Is it *my* fault that my mother and I are being sent to live in the desert? If my father really loved me, would he abandon my mother and me and send us away to uncertain futures?

When I read Ishmael's story I wonder if he, like so many teens today, carried with him feelings of guilt, rejection, anger, and sadness because of his broken relationship with his father. Ishmael wasn't a bad child when he was sent away, and he had spent meaningful time with his father. Was Ishmael ever angry with God? It seems that he had every reason to be. After all, why did God allow this to happen?

The truth is that Abraham loved both of his sons. Abraham let Ishmael go only after God promised him that Ishmael would be blessed, too. God told Abraham, "Isaac will inherit your family name, but the son of the slave woman is also your son, and I will make his descendants into a great nation" (Genesis 21:12 CEV).

The comforting knowledge that he would one day found a nation wasn't available to Ishmael. Even if Ishmael knew the prophecy, the distant future can be impossible to imagine when you are young and hungry and afraid. The truth is that Ishmael probably felt like a lot of teenager people. He was probably furious that he and his mother had been kicked out of their comfortable home. He undoubtedly thought that his father hated him, which may have made him hate himself. Most likely he was sad that his mother had to work so hard to make a decent life for him. Certainly Ishmael had lots of unanswered questions.

But here is the first thing that I would tell Ishmael. This is exactly what I wish someone had told me when my father left me when I was three years old: "What happened to you was not your fault, and you definitely didn't deserve it!" I would tell Ishmael to look carefully at the details of his life; a close look always makes it clear how much God loves each of us. God cared deeply for Ishmael. Because the Lord watches over us, God knew the details of Ishmael's life; God had a promise and a plan for Ishmael's life. Though it might not have always felt to Ishmael like there was a plan, God had Ishmael's back! This is how God works. The Lord looked to Ishmael's future and didn't focus on his family's failures. Now, that should be encouraging to you. Instead of thinking about failures, consider that you may have big obstacles that you must learn to overcome. God can take whatever you have been through and use you for a greater purpose.

As for our issues with our parents, the challenge of getting older is that at some point we have to forgive them. If you look at Genesis 25:7-11, you will see that Ishmael was there when Abraham died. Ishmael and Isaac buried their father, which suggests that Ishmael found a way to overcome the pain of what happened when he was a child and was able to forgive his father for what he had done. If

> If you want to have a good life, there is no choice other than learning to forgive those who hurt you.

you want to have a good life, there is no choice other than learning to forgive those who hurt you. Parents are as human and flawed as the rest of us. And while the way that they raised us was not perfect and may have been harmful, it was clearly all that they knew how to do. That is hard to hear. But drugs and alcohol, mental illness, ignorance, and selfishness cloud good decision-making and choosing to do the right thing. Anger sends us down the same road that trapped our parents. It keeps us from being our best selves. It keeps us from living into God's gifts for us.

Sometimes the questions we have for our parents will never be answered. You are justified in being angry, confused, or sad, and God is God enough to handle your anger, clear up your confusion, and heal your sadness. But the way to heal and overcome the pain is to know that regardless of what happened to you, you made it through. The reason that you made it through the pain and problems was because God had something more planned for you. God is focused on your future, not on the flaws in your family. You can spend time thinking about how difficult and unfair your life has been,

> **God is focused on your future, not on the flaws in your family.**

but that's not what God wants for you. God wants the same thing for you that he wanted for Ishmael: He wants a spectacular and triumphant future. He wants you to be a leader—in your own life and in ways that involve your spiritual gifts. So stop focusing on the flaws in your family. Stop focusing on what is wrong with you. Start seeing yourself as God's graffiti—good enough as you are, smart enough and talented enough to do whatever it is that you set your mind to do. Start focusing on God's plans for your future.

You Are Not a Mistake; You're a Miracle

While some preachers and scholars have suggested that Ishmael should never have been born, that it was a mistake for Sarah and Abraham to use Hagar to create a son instead of waiting for God's timing, that isn't how Abraham or God seemed to view Ishmael. You can be certain that God doesn't view you as a mistake, no matter what the circumstances of your birth. The psalmist understood this when he said:

> I praise you because I am fearfully and
>   wonderfully made;
> your works are wonderful,
> I know that full well.
> —Psalm 139:14

Believe God's Word and believe in yourself! What evidence do we have that you are a miracle? God made you! You are

God's child. And God doesn't make mistakes. That is all you need to know.

Before Ishmael was aware of God's presence in his life, God loved Ishmael. Before Ishmael was unable to form words, God had heard his voice. There is a lesson in this: God provides for us because God loves us, as God loved Ishmael. God does not care if we are rich or poor, what neighborhood we claim as home, or what race or gender we are. God cares for us because we are all made in God's image; we are God's children. No matter what happens in our lives, God pays attention to our needs. When Ishmael cried, God heard and responded (Genesis 21:15-17).

Some of us are taught that we have to be in terrible condition for God to respond to us. We might have been told that we have to engage in certain behaviors for God to pay attention to us—for example, we have to pray certain ways or spend a certain amount of time in church. The truth is, God requires only that we believe.

In Hebrew, the name Ishmael means "God hears." Ishmael's name is a reminder to us that we can cry out to the Lord at any time we have need of God's presence. God hears and responds to our cries for help. If Ishmael could look back over his life and tell his story today, this is what I think he would say to us:

> **God hears and responds to our cries for help.**

My name is Ishmael. I am father of the Arab people. That is where I ended up.

This is how I started: My mother, Hagar, lived in the house of Sarah and Abraham. She was a handmaid to Sarah. Sarah was barren until she was an elderly woman and gave birth to her son Issac. I must admit that I was a bit jealous of him, and I guess it showed because his mother caught me laughing at her son. Sarah didn't like me laughing at him, and it made her so angry that she told my father to send my mother and me away.

Because I led a great nation just as God promised my father, Abraham, I know that generations of people will tell the more complicated details of the story of my life. All that you need to know is this: One day I cried aloud in the wilderness; God heard my cry, and he will hear you too.

What Are Our Closing Thoughts on Ishmael?

Ishmael, son of Abraham and Hagar, was born into a situation that became very difficult. The Lord spoke to Hagar: "You are now pregnant, and you will give birth to a son. You shall name him Ishmael" (Genesis 16:11). Throughout his later life, Ishmael had to get comfortable anywhere and everywhere. And though he had a bad start, Ishmael became the inheritor of a kingdom.

So what does this have to do with you? It means that you, like Ishmael, may have had an unfair start, but it's not your fault. God hears you. God has a plan for your life and wishes only the best for you. How you start does not have to determine how you finish. Believe in yourself; trust God, dream, and dream big! Deal with your anger about what you have gone through by seeking the support of people who care about you. Learn to love yourself, and allow others to love you.

Beginning: Ishmael was the disregarded son of a slave.
Ending: Ishmael became the father of a nation.
What made the difference: Even though Ishmael was born into challenging circumstances because of choices made by his parents, God still loved Ishmael and had a purpose for his life. The choices made by your parents can't stop God from using you for a purpose.

What Now?

The following are activities that can be completed and questions that can be answered in Christian education classes or Bible study or written as answers in a journal that records your spiritual journey.

1. When you don't understand who you are, question your talents, are not sure of your purpose, or are not sure what you want to do with your life, it will make you fear the future. Do you have any fears about what the future holds for you? List three of your fears below.
   a.
   b.
   c.
2. What is the source of your fear?
3. It's easy to spend your life angry with the people who hurt you and blame others for why life is so hard or, even worse, spending your life seeking revenge or trying to punish

those who hurt you, but all of these things get in the way of finding your true purpose in life. Who are you still angry with because of what happened to you?

4. How can you let go of the anger so that it doesn't hold you back and keep you from experiencing God's purpose for your life?

5. Go back over the causes and symptoms of low self-esteem. Write down any causes and symptoms that relate to you. How will you work to address the causes and symptoms so that you can feel better about yourself?

6. Think about your future. What are your life goals (personal and career)? What do you want the world to know about you?

Get Prayed Up

Dear God, my family has challenges, my life is not perfect, and I have been angry about a lot of things. God, I need you to help me overcome the anger. My parents' decisions are not my fault, and I need you to help me remember that I have a great purpose. I need your help to find my purpose. Because of what I've been through I don't always feel good about myself. God, please help me overcome my self-esteem issues. Please send people into my life who can inspire me to believe in myself. Please continue to protect my heart, my goals, my dreams, and my family. Amen.

Notes
1. The name Ishmael means "God hears."
2. In this sense, the word "reckoned" means that Isaac will

be shown to be of considerable importance.

3. The patriarch is the head of the family, the heir (inheritor) of lands and the family fortune.

4. Sun Tzu, *The Art of War*, Ch. 3.

5. For more information about forms of child abuse, see http://www.childhelp.org/pages/satatistics (accessed April 23, 2012).

6. "Bullying," *American Academy of Child and Adolescent Psychiatry* 80 (March 2011), http://www.aacap.org/cs/root/facts_for_families/bullying (accessed April 23, 2012).

7. "Teens: Alcohol and Other Drugs," *American Academy of Child and Adolescent Psychiatry* 3 ([updated] March 2011), http://aacap.org/page.ww?name=Teens:+Alcohol+and+Other+Drugs&section=Facts+for+Families (accessed April 30, 2012).

8. "Eating Disorders Statistics," http://www.anad.org/get-information/about-eating-disorders-statistics (accessed April 23, 2012).

9. "Teen Suicide Overview," http://www.teensuicidestatistics.com/ (accessed April 23, 2012).

5

Hagar

You Are Not Alone

Ending: God provided for Hagar's needs, and her son became the father of a nation.

Beginning: A single mom, Hagar had to take care of her son by herself.

Scripture doesn't tell us exactly how Hagar ended up with Abraham and Sarah. Other religions have traditions and stories about how Hagar came to be with Abraham and Sarah. All the Christian Bible tells us is that she was a slave in the household of Abraham, that she was servant to Sarah, his wife, and that she was an Egyptian. Christian tradition thinks that Hagar was probably sold into slavery as a girl, most likely a spoil of war who was either orphaned or kidnapped.

In the following passage of Scripture, any respect between Sarah and Hagar ended up as resentment and hostility on the part of Sarah. She said to Abraham, "Get rid of that Egyptian slave woman and her son! I don't want him to inherit anything. It should all go to my son" (Genesis 21:10 CEV). Abraham did what Sarah wanted and sent Hagar and Ishmael away. Hagar had to raise Ishmael on her own.

It's hard growing up in a single-parent home. Sometimes you spend very little time with your mother because she is working hard to make sure that she is able to provide for you. As a result she is not always able to give you all of the attention that you need or want. When I was a very small child, at the age of three, my dad left my mom. My mother was only seventeen years old when she had me. She hadn't finished high school yet and had to figure out how to take care of herself and me. Making sure we would be okay took up a lot of her time. She had to work, go to night school, and take care of me as a child. On top of all that she was only a teenager and wanted to find time to be like other young women her age. I imagine it was pretty hard for my mom as a young woman, and it was just as hard if not harder for Hagar.

Evicted from her home, even if it was a home provided by slavery, Hagar found herself alone with a young child, wandering in the wilderness with only the supplies she could carry. And when you see "wilderness," you should read "desert." It was hot and dry with limited vegetation for food, and water was hard to find. Naturally, Hagar was concerned about how she and her son were going to make it on their own. She didn't know how she was would be able to provide basic food and shelter, much less protection from any wild animals or human threats they might encounter. Can you imagine how that must have felt—a woman alone in the desert with only a young boy for company? Maybe you can!

Maybe you've survived something similar yourself. You or someone you know may be going through a desert experience caring for a child, feeling alone and helpless. Don't give up or lose hope. God is a provider.

Don't give up or lose hope. God is a provider.

If you are growing up with just your mom to take care of you, you may sometimes wonder why your mother is stressed out, always tired, and working so hard. It's because she is trying to make sure that the two of you are okay. She is worried about paying the bills to keep a roof over your heads, the electricity turned on, and food on the table, not to mention she is trying to ensure your safety and success in life. Most of the time our parent would love to spend more time with us, but because of the situation, she (or he) spends a lot of time making sure the family is going to be okay.

In this situation Hagar wasn't sure what was going to happen. The Bible says that when Abraham sent Hagar and Ishmael away, they were homeless and alone. "Early the next morning Abraham gave Hagar an animal skin full of water and some bread. Then he put the boy on her shoulder and sent them away. They wandered around in the desert near Beersheba" (Genesis 21:14 CEV). There she was on her own with no one to turn to for help. She had no job and no money. Hagar was alone and afraid. It didn't look like she and her son were going to make it. The Bible says, "When the water in the skin was gone, she put the boy under one of the bushes. Then she went off and sat down about a bowshot away, for she thought, 'I cannot watch the boy die.' And as she sat there, she began to sob" (Genesis 21:15-16).

The Process of Provision

> When God heard the boy crying, the angel of God called out to Hagar from heaven and said, "Hagar, why are you worried? Don't be afraid. I have heard your son crying. Help him up and hold his hand, because I will make him the father of a great nation." (Genesis 21:17-18 CEV)

Hagar shows us that survival is possible even under the hardest conditions. Hagar couldn't bear the thought of watching her child suffer. But God helped Hagar put her priorities back in order. God wanted her to understand that her son was the most important part of her life; she needed to snap out of her depression, confusion, and anger and focus on making life better for both of them. Sometimes the key to turning around a bad situation is not to panic; instead regroup, get your priorities in order and look to God for guidance. Depression, fear and anxiety can cloud your judgment and cause you to miss solutions that are right in front you, but you couldn't see them because you were distracted by worry. When fear and worry consume your thoughts it's hard to figure out solutions. That's why you have to resist the temptation to focus on the problem and remember that you have purpose. When you are focused on your purpose you become determined to solve the problem. God will not let you miss out on your purpose because of a problem. You just have to turn to the Lord for help.

Survival is possible even under the hardest conditions.

God told Hagar to lift Ishmael out of the bush in which she had put him and to hold Ishmael's hand (Genesis 21:18). Even when a parent has nothing of material value to give, he or she still has the ability to show love. Before God showed her how to make provision for Ishmael, he showed Hagar what Ishmael needed most. Like all of us, what Ishmael needed most was for his mother to show him love and comfort no matter how tough things got for them. When a parent and child are linked together in this way, there is no challenge they cannot overcome. Lifting Ishmael up by the hand was also a way of letting him know that she was present and ready to lead them in a new direction.

It wasn't easy growing up not knowing my father, and raising me on her own was a challenge for my mom. Like Hagar and Ishmael, we were poor and my mom was young. A lot of kids grow up in this situation, and sometimes people on the outside look at us and don't think we will amount to much. But the good thing is that other people don't have the power to decide what happens to me or to you. Only God does.

For Every Obstacle God Has an Opportunity

"I will make him into a great nation." (Genesis 21:18)

When Abraham sent Hagar and her son away, it was definitely not a good thing. Hagar was alone and vulnerable, unprotected and unprovided for. She was at the mercy of the elements and of enemies, both animal and human, which might see a woman and child alone as ripe picking. Like any young mother caring for her children alone, there are the dangers of people who want to take advantage of a vulnerable situation. But if she *could* survive, what then? In letting her go, Abraham had also set her free: Hagar was no longer a slave.

Yes, it was hard being a single mom, but freedom also created an opportunity for Hagar; it was an opportunity to make her own decisions about how she wanted to live her life. Sometimes when God removes you from a situation that wasn't good for you, you find yourself wishing you were still in that situation—because at least you would not be alone. But God doesn't want you to be taken advantage of or abused by anyone. You deserve better. Being alone

> **God doesn't want you to be taken advantage of or abused by anyone. You deserve better.**

doesn't mean you have to be lonely. God is with you, and God has brought you out of the situation because God knows that you deserve better.

When Abraham sent Hagar away, it freed her from being controlled by him or subjected to the abuse of Sarah. Hagar was able to experience life on her own terms—not only for herself but also for her son. God had a plan for her son's life. The angel told her that God would make her son into a great nation. That meant that her son had a future. He would be okay, and she would be okay.

Sarah may have thought she was hurting Hagar and Ishmael by making Abraham send them away. Sarah may have even thought their banishment was a death sentence. How could a woman and child survive alone in the wilderness? It looked like their lives were over, but God had a different plan. The Bible says that Hagar returned with

God doesn't make false promises.

Ishmael to Egypt, her homeland. Ishmael ultimately married and had twelve sons of his own—and they, like the sons of Isaac, became a mighty nation, just as God had promised (Genesis 21:20-21; 25:12-13).

On that day in the wilderness, when Hagar was lost in despair, God told Hagar not to be afraid. The Lord was going to make sure they would be okay. God doesn't make false promises, and as evidence that life was going to get better, the Bible says that God started providing right away. "Then God opened her eyes and she saw a well of water. So she went and filled the skin with water and gave the boy a drink" (Genesis 21:19). From that moment on life began to change—for the better.

Once Hagar listened to God, the Lord gave her the promise for Ishmael's future. Hagar had to show God *and* Ishmael that she was willing to trust God and be present to her son. In the same way, if you are growing up with just you and your mom, God is present and able to take care of both of you. God hears your cry just like God heard Ishmael crying and sent an angel to Hagar. There will always be people in life who are like angels. These angels are the people who encourage your mother to keep going, keep believing, and never give up. God uses people to do this because God has a greater purpose for both of you. Angels are the people who allow God to use them and speak words of encouragement into our lives.

God showed Hagar that she was not alone. She was going to have divine assistance in taking care of Ishmael. God is also there for your mother, helping her take care of you so that you can continue to grow into the person that God created you to be and do that things in life that God created you to do.

When Hagar listened to God and believed what God said, that's when God opened her eyes to see the opportunity in front of her: "Then God opened her eyes and she saw a well of water" (Genesis 21:19). You may be growing up in a single-parent home, but you are not alone. God is there to help you. Keep trusting God, and God will open your eyes to the opportunities on the other side of the obstacles.

Beginning: A single mom, Hagar had to take care of her son by herself.

Ending: God provided for Hagar's needs, and her son became the father of a nation.

What made the difference: Hagar trusted God and believed God's promise to take care of her and Ishmael. She did what God asked her to do, and that's when God was able to open her eyes to opportunities on the other side of the obstacles.

What Now?

The following are activities that can be completed and questions that can be answered in Christian education classes or Bible study or written as answers in a journal that records your spiritual journey.

1. God showed Hagar that for every obstacle there is an opportunity. Hagar couldn't see the water that was right there because she was focused on the obstacles. What obstacles in your life are you giving so much attention that they are keeping you from seeing the opportunities? List them below.

a.

b.

c.

2. How can you overcome the obstacles, or what can you do so that they don't distract you from the opportunities?

3. It was undoubtedly hard for Hagar as a single mom. It surely took a lot of work to make sure Ishmael would be okay, but I imagine that sometimes he needed her attention or wanted her to hug him and hold his hand. Sometimes we need attention from our parent, and even though it may be hard to ask, it's worth it when we do. How would you like your parent to spend more time with you, showing that they love you, talking to you about your dreams and the things you want to do in life? Write down what you would say to your parent if you were not afraid, and then pray and ask God to give you the courage to tell your mom or dad what you really want.

4. What are some things that you would like to do with your mom? Places you'd like to go together? Or things you would like to hear your mother say that would make you feel better? List them below.

Three things I'd like to do with my mom:

a.

b.

c.

Three places I'd like to go with my mom:

a.

b.

c.

Three things I wish my mom would say:

a.

b.

c.

5. How can you help your mom and make her life a little less stressful? How can you show her that you love her and understand that it's not easy for her? List some ideas for what you can do below.

a.

b.

c.

Get Prayed Up

God, my mom is raising me on her own, but I know that we are not alone and you are with us. Thank you, God, for meeting our needs during those times when we have felt like we were in the wilderness with no place to turn. Sometimes life gets hard for us, and my mother and I are still afraid of what the future holds. Help us to overcome the fear so that we can see beyond the obstacles and find the opportunities. Please give my mother strength, peace, and happiness, because she deserves it and works so hard to provide for us. And thank you, God, for giving both of us a bright future. Thank you for keeping your promise and making sure that we are okay. Amen.

6

Esther

God's Purpose for You May Surprise You

Ending: Queen Esther saved her family members and community from danger.

Beginning: Esther, a young orphan girl, was raised by her cousin and lived in exile in a foreign land.

Mordecai had a very beautiful cousin named Esther, whose Hebrew name was Hadassah. He had raised her as his own daughter, after her father and mother died. (Esther 2:7 CEV)

Esther's story is quite fantastic. She was a Jew, named Hadassah by her parents, who died when she was very young. The Bible doesn't tell us about that tragedy. Were her parents killed during the Babylonian exile under the reign of Nebuchadnezzar II? Perhaps she lost them to disease or poor living conditions. Or perhaps she lost her mother (unnamed) in childbirth and her father, Abihail, to another natural cause. We don't know for sure. We know only that

Hadassah became an orphan and was taken in by a cousin (uncle in other Bible versions), a man named Mordecai, who adopted her as his daughter after her parents' deaths.

The biblical story finds Hadassah, who has taken the Persian name of Esther, and Mordecai living in the Persian capital city of Susa. (Babylon had fallen to Persia, and thus the Jewish exiles came under the rule of a new foreign power.) Esther and Mordecai seem to have a devoted relationship, built on loving respect. But Esther, with all the young women of the city, was compelled to participate in a royal beauty pageant and sent to live in the harem of the Persian king.

Perhaps you, like Esther, don't have parents involved in your lives. Their absence may be due to work, divorce, a history of abusive behavior, prison, or death. Perhaps the adults who are in your life are as devoted, protective, and generous like Mordecai was to Esther. But not all of us have that particular blessing. I had that kind of presence in my grandmother, but my relationship with my father was more than a bit complicated.

Working Past Forgiveness

You'll remember that my father abandoned my mother and me when I was very young. I had a lot of anger about that abandonment, for my own sake and for my mom's. Part of the anger was self-directed because I, like many young people, secretly feared that I was the reason my dad had left. Maybe it was my fault in some way that my parents hadn't been able to make their relationship work.

When I was a teenager, my father and I had the opportunity to meet again. I even went to live with him during my high school years. As happy as I was to get to know him better, our time together was tough. The house was filled with free-floating anger. I was still angry with my father for having abandoned me. He blamed my mother for why he was not able to be around when I was growing up. As far as I was concerned, even with all of her problems, my mother had stuck around when my father ran away. His blaming her infuriated me.

My dad and I never really reconciled. After graduation I moved out of his house and decided to figure out life on my own. With a lot of counseling and time to reflect on the best direction for my life, I came to realize that my father loved me, but he was not able to give me the kind of love that I needed. Holding on to anger about that was only hurting me. Letting go of anger allowed me to forgive my father and start to heal. I understood that being abandoned by my father had not happened because I was a flawed child but because he was a scared and scarred man. Abandonment did not define me. My parents' behavior did not create my destiny. Remember what Malachy McCourt said? "Resentment is like taking poison and waiting for the other person to die." I no longer needed to hold on to anger. Holding on to anger wasn't going to hurt anyone but me. I finally started to believe that I was worthy of love. I focused on God's plan for my life.

I wonder if Esther ever felt angry with Mordecai for letting her be carried off from their home and sent to the king's palace. It must have been terrifying for her to be alone in a strange place. Did she ever feel abandoned by her adoptive father? Such feelings would have been all too natural.

It does seem that Mordecai was able to support Esther through the experience. Even though Mordecai couldn't stop the separation, he didn't abandon Esther. He stayed as close as he could. Every day, he would stroll by the courtyard of the king's harem (Esther 2:11). Somehow, he would catch a glimpse of his daughter or get a report about her well-being. And they found a way to pass messages back and forth, even after Esther was made queen.

Learning from Pain to Fulfill Your Purpose

Perhaps by now you've figured out that Esther's story was anything but a Cinderella story. The poor little orphan girl may have ended up as royalty, but there was high risk involved—and no choice. She was removed from her home and placed in a luxurious prison—the king's harem. She had no privacy and was not allowed to have an opinion on what she was going through. Then she was one of a long string of one-night stands with the king. If she hadn't been chosen as queen, she probably would have suffered in the harem for life, ineligible to marry any other man and unable to return home to Mordecai. And that was all before she approached the king to speak for the Jewish people, and, as a result, outing herself as one of them.

Esther's situation was a challenging one. But her life teaches us that no matter what our circumstances, God can use us to do great things. As Mordecai counseled Esther, God creates and defines each of us to live out a unique purpose. Parents

are supposed to have a role in that journey, but when they can't or won't, God's
plan doesn't change. God just changes
how the plan gets done.

> No matter what our circumstances, God can use us to do great things.

All of us are the products of our pasts.
Pain cannot be completely avoided. But
whether that pain includes the absence of
our parents or the consequences of our own behaviors, we
don't have to be prisoners of personal pain. What aspects of
Esther's painful story can you identify with? We are all going
to experience some measure of pain many times in our lives.
So, how do we manage it? How do you learn from pain so
that you are able to fulfill God's purpose for your lives?

1. *Be honest about your feelings.* Accept the reality that
you are sad and hurt and lonely.

2. *Get someone in your corner.* Talk to someone who can
understand your deepest and most personal thoughts and
feelings.

3. *Talk to God.* Ask God for strength to manage and overcome your pain.

4. *Connect your past and present pain.* Understand how pain
from your past will affect your behavior unless it is resolved.

Don't Hide Who You Are

Esther had a complicated life. She was a religious and ethnic
minority, living as a second- or third-generation immigrant
in a strange land. She wouldn't have had any personal
memories of the Jewish homeland, but she would have heard

> **Hiding who you are keeps you from fulfilling your purpose. God created you as God meant you to be.**

the stories. Mordecai clearly raised her with a strong sense of her Jewish identity—but then he insisted on secrecy about that identity (Esther 2:10). It wasn't safe, especially in the king's palace, to reveal that she was a Jew.

If your parents or other relatives are undocumented immigrants in this country, you will have a strong sense of the kind of pressure, fear, and danger such need for secrecy inspires. It may not be you but you may have a friend who can relate to what it's like having to hide who you are. Like today's immigrant parents, Mordecai knew that if the government knew about Esther's nationality or orphan status, she would be vulnerable—and possibly even in danger.

We all know that people will judge us based on where we live, how we look, who our parents are, the color of our skin, the language that we speak, how well we speak, our educational status or citizenship, and if we have been in trouble with the law. Mordecai wanted to give Esther the best shot at being accepted, so he told her to hide her true identity. But that strategy never works in the long-term. Hiding who you are keeps you from fulfilling your purpose. God created you as God meant you to be. The Lord does not use imposters.

When I was young, we moved every year. There was always a challenge to be accepted because every neighborhood was different; each one treated outsiders differently and had different expectations of the people they let into their circle of friends. Their rules changed based on how you looked, dressed, and talked. Each neighborhood evaluated how much money you had and if you lived with one or both of your parents. Depending on the community's opinions you were liked or disliked, respected or disrespected, weak or an equal.

During my high school years, kids in my neighborhood were bused across town to attend school. The school was in a middle-class neighborhood that was predominantly white and Asian. Most kids hung out with students who looked like them, dressed liked them, and lived where they lived. I was surprised to discover that students from my new school liked me and wanted to spend time with me. They assumed that I lived in a middle-class neighborhood similar to theirs. I hung out with them for a few weeks. One day they offered me a ride home. I knew that if they found out where I lived, they would no longer want me around. I also knew that they offered me a ride home only because they wanted to see where I lived and what my house looked like.

I accepted the ride home, but while in the car I made a strategic decision. I decided not to have them drive me to the house that I shared with my grandmother. Our neighborhood, which was poor, sat near a nice middle-class community. I had them drop me off just close enough for me to walk the remaining distance but not so close that they would be able to determine that I lived in the poor neighborhood. My ruse didn't work; they started asking around at school and learned the truth. Just as I thought, when they found out where I lived, they laughed at me and we no longer were friends.

That experience is an example of the terrible cruelty some of us experience as teenagers. But adults also do the same kind of thing all the time. I've had similar experiences as an adult dealing with politicians, church folk, and sometimes even people who look like me who attempt to use my poor childhood and mistakes against me. Kids who treat other kids that way too often grow up to be adults who do the same thing. And the important thing to know is that our experiences do shape us. But we can choose the shape of our own destinies. There is nothing wrong with not having a lot of money, but there is something sad about deciding that no money equals no self-worth. On the flip side, lots of money does not equal self-worth. We must determine who we are and who we want to be. We cannot hide from ourselves or from God.

> Our experiences do shape us. But we can choose the shape of our own destinies.

Too many young people start out life thinking about what they want to become in life based on what they want to have in life. We hardly ever plan to have lives and careers that will allow us to have joy, peace, fulfillment, and balance. We typically think about careers that will allow us to buy things that we hope will give us joy, peace, and fulfillment. Later in life we learn that these things can't be purchased.

Hiding who you are works for only a little while. God created you to be who you are and to live fully and unapologetically. Don't be ashamed of who you are because of what other people might think of you.

Some people will reject you because of who they think that you might be or might become. This, is only a sign that they are not the people God plans to use in your life. They cannot help you fulfill your purpose. God always sends the right people to solve a problem. God always sends the right people to help you fulfill your purpose.

When people reject you, it's only a sign that they are not the people God plans to use in your self.

That was true in Esther's case. She was raised by her cousin as his own daughter. Mordecai raised her to be an exceptional young woman. And in her palace prison, that exceptional young woman impressed everyone who met her. The king's servant who was in charge of all the harem women took a special interest in her, advised her, and befriended her. Esther's character as well as her beauty ultimately won not only the passion but also the respect of the king. She may have kept her Jewish ethnicity a secret for a time, but the rest of her family's legacy—of faith and integrity—shone through clear and bright!

When I finally decided to stop worrying about what other people thought, acting the way they wanted me to act, and doing what they wanted me to do, I was able to start living out my purpose. My purpose was to help young people whose lives were very similar to mine.

When you look at Esther's story, her purpose was to help not only herself but also her people. That's why, although Mordecai advised her to keep her Jewish identity secret for a time, there also came a day when he told her, "It may be that *you*—in all of your strong, beautiful, Jewish self—were born for just a time as this." Esther gathered all her courage (because going uninvited before the king was incredibly dangerous) and put her life on the line.

Esther put a strategy into place, utilizing her political savvy, her natural intellect, and her beauty to lure the king, and then she said plainly, "Your Majesty, if you really care for me and are willing to help, you can save me and my people. That's what I really want" (Esther 7:3 CEV). Esther understood that true purpose in life is not about helping yourself but also helping the people in your community. God did not give her favor with the king to help herself but so that she could help her people. When she went to the king with her request, she made the case for her community to be spared by saying, "You can save me only if you save them, because I am one of them."

There are strategies for living beyond the boundaries of your circumstances in pursuit of your dreams. Life won't ever be easy. Mine hasn't been, for sure. But my life has been rewarding; I have a sense of inner peace knowing that I am free to be myself and do what I believe God created me to do. God wants the same thing for you that God wanted for Esther: to stop hiding who she was and to be courageous enough to stand up for the people who need you—your family, community, friends, and yourself. When you make the decision to be unapologetically yourself and to do the things that you know in your heart are right, that's what gives you inner peace and the ability to go out and do what God created you to do.

There are lots of people who have trouble finding their purposes in life. Even though many us follow educational and career paths that give us social and monetary rewards designed to help us live the good life, many of us spend time feeling like imposters in our own lives. There is even an imposter syndrome, which describes people who don't feel good enough about themselves and are fearful that someone will find out that they are faking the qualities that brought them their success, good qualities, or other benefits worth acknowledging.

> **True purpose in life is not about helping yourself but also helping the people in your community.**

God created you to do something that no one can do but you. You have gifts and talents that make you uniquely different from anyone else on earth. There are people whose lives will be changed because of your story, experiences, and victories. No one else can deliver your message because know one else knows your story better than you do. There are people waiting to hear your voice and to learn from your journey. They are waiting for you to show up. You just have to believe in yourself and have the courage to try.

Find Your Place

> Everyone liked Esther. . . . Xerxes liked Esther more than he did any of the other young women. None of them pleased him as much as she did, and right away he fell in love with her and crowned her queen in place of Vashti. (Esther 2:15,17 CEV)

For much of her life Esther felt out of place. She had no parents, she lived in exile, and she could not claim who she was. Even with all of this against her, everyone liked Esther.

God loves you and is determined to see you live out your purpose.

That included the king. As a result, the king chose her as his new queen (after demoting his previous wife, Vashti, when she offended his pride by refusing to come when he called; see Esther 1). It didn't seem like it at the time, but when Esther was brought to the palace and ultimately made queen, everything was working in Esther's favor and toward her bigger purpose.

Throughout my life there have been people who saw leadership qualities in me that I didn't see in myself. There were many who believed in my potential even though my behaviors could have caused a lot of people to turn away from me. My behavior and bad attitude were easy to diagnose: I was seeking the attention that I wasn't getting at home. Fortunately for me there were adults who could see that my behavior was just an expression of my pain.

Here is the good news! God loves you and is determined to see you live out your purpose. You may take some strange paths on the way there but you will get there. To keep us on track, God will send angels—people who love, guide, and support us. So many of us are so used to rejection that we don't recognize help when we see it. We're almost hardwired to reject people when they show concern for us. We have a choice about how we respond to other people when God shows them our value. Nothing you've been through in life is so bad that you don't deserve to be treated well. God wants you to experience what it's like to be loved, appreciated, and treated with respect just because you are God's child.

Find Your Purpose

"It could be that you were made queen for a time like this!" (Esther 4:14 CEV)

Purpose is always bigger than you are. Purpose is about how you are going to help the people who need you and the specific kind of support and service that is your gift. While God wants you to have a better life, to be treated well, and to live the life of your dreams, God does this so that you can pay it forward. Being a child of God involves opening doors for people who are just like you, who are wondering if life is ever going to get better.

That's the reason why God wants you to find your purpose. When you find your purpose you now have the map to help other people navigate their way through the challenges to experience what God has for them. You didn't make it by yourself. People helped you along the way, and God wants you to be courageous enough to overcome the pain, to forgive, and to celebrate what God has done in your life, and then ask God how he wants to use you to help others who are still enduring the pain that you have learned to overcome.

Take the Risk If You Want the Reward

When Mordecai offended the Persian king's second-in-command, that official made a plot to kill all of the Jews living in Persia. He didn't know that Esther, the new queen, was Jewish and that Mordecai was her adoptive father. Esther had kept this secret from everyone, including her royal husband. But now Mordecai asked Esther to report the official's plot to the king, stating, "If you remain silent at this time, relief and deliverance for the Jews will arise from another place, but you and your father's family will perish. And who knows but that you have come to royal position for such a time as this?" (Esther 4:14).

To get involved in this situation put Esther's life in extreme danger. If she spoke out, she'd have to survive having disobeyed a rule of the court, because no one was to approach the king unless invited to do so. And her reason for approaching him was to talk about a dangerous topic. Esther was afraid of what might happen, and this is the message she sent back:

> "Tell Mordecai there is a law about going in to see the king, and all his officials and his people know about this law. Anyone who goes in to see the king without being invited by him will be put to death. The only way that anyone can be saved is for the king to hold out the gold scepter to that person. And it's been thirty days since he has asked for me." (Esther 4:10-11 CEV)

In addition to the dangers involved with approaching the king, there was still the issue of revealing her true identity. But Mordecai wasn't satisfied with her answer; he wanted her to know that fear was not a good excuse and worrying about herself was not good enough. She should be concerned

about the lives of the people from her community (Esther 4:12-14).

Esther knew that there are times when
it is essential to stand up for oneself. Saving her people, the Jews, was Esther's pur-

Life doesn't get easier, but it does get better.

pose. When God is trying to move you into your purpose,
it's never about what you can do alone; it's about what God
can do with you. As Esther did, it is important to confront
your fears and be courageous enough to trust that God will
see you through even the most difficult decisions. Esther
loved her cousin and the people in her community. Esther
chose love over fear. In her next message to Mordecai, she
said, "Go, gather together all the Jews who are in Susa, and
fast for me. Do not eat or drink for three days, night or day.
I and my attendants will fast as you do. When this is done,
I will go to the king, even though it is against the law. And
if I perish, I perish" (Esther 4:15-16).

Life doesn't get easier, but it does get better. There is wonderful victory in trying to, and in overcoming fear. A lot of
people never even try. Your efforts and courage separate you
from people who do what they've always done and are surprised that nothing changes.

Esther went to her husband, the king. She spoke up for
her adoptive father and the people of her community. In
the end, the Jews were saved from harm, and in a note of
comic irony, the second-in-command was executed on the
gallows he had built for Mordecai, while Mordecai himself was promoted by the king to fill the vacancy. "Mordecai the Jew was second in rank to King Xerxes,
preeminent among the Jews, and he was held in high

esteem by his many fellow Jews, because he worked for the good of his people and spoke up for the welfare of all the Jews" (Esther 10:3).

Your life has purpose. God will use you for that purpose. Your purpose will always help other people through gifts that you know and those that you develop to meet a special need. What is required of each of us? Willing and open hearts and trust in God. It is just that simple.

Beginning: Esther, a young orphan girl, was raised by her cousin and lived in exile in a foreign land.

Ending: Queen Esther saved her family members and community from danger.

What made the difference: Esther chose to be courageous enough to help her family and her community even if it meant risking her own safety. As a result of her courage she saved herself and her people and no longer had to hide who she was. Esther was finally free to be herself.

What Now?

The following are activities that can be completed and questions that can be answered in Christian education classes or Bible study or written as answers in a journal that records your spiritual journey.

1. When you look at your life and compare it with Esther's, are there things about yourself that you are hiding because you are afraid of what other people will think of you? What are they?

2. What would it take for you to overcome your fear of what other people think so that you can start living the life that you deserve?

3. Are there people you know who would be helped by your decision to be yourself? Who are they?

4. As was the case for Esther, God has an amazing purpose for your life. There are things in life that only you can do, but you have to be yourself and unafraid to try. What are three things you believe that you were created to do? Think about what you are good at, and let that be your guide for answering the question.

a.

b.

c.

5. What would you do if you knew you wouldn't fail? Remember that the thing you fear most is the thing least likely to happen.

Get Prayed Up

Dear God, give me sense of purpose, vision, and courage. Sometimes I am afraid to be myself because of what other people might think, and I end up doing what pleases them. It makes me feel terrible on the inside. God, I want to be freed from worrying about what other people think so that I can have inner peace and live the life that you have for me. I believe that my life has purpose, and I know that I need your help to find. Guide me through the challenges, and help me overcome fear so that I can always do the right thing even when it is not popular. God, I want to please you. I know that when people in my family see me trying and being my-self, it will inspire them to do the same. Help me to change my life so that I can help others change their lives. Show me what it is you want me to do, and then help me find the words to speak when you need me to speak up. I know that if I trust you to guide me, I will have peace. Amen.

7

Joseph

Dream Your Own Dream

Ending: Joseph was a leader who saved his family and community during a famine.

Beginning: Joseph was rejected by his brothers, had problems with his father, and was thrown in jail for a crime he didn't commit.

I imagine that people in Joseph's community thought that Joseph's family had a good life. His father was well-respected. Joseph and his brothers were doing well in their professions. They looked like a perfect family—but this was a terribly dysfunctional family with problems similar to those of so many other families.

Sometimes we look at the lives of other people and say, "I wish my family were like that," or "If I had the same advantages that they have, my life would be so much better." But we never know what life is like for other people. All of us have our challenges. It is how we face and overcome our challenges that makes the difference in our lives. When Joseph faced his family challenges, he made a series of choices that had a devastating effect on his life.

Sometimes the people closest to us have the ability to hurt us the most. This is because these are the people we love and the people who are supposed to love us. Naturally, we have higher expectations of them than we tend to have of people outside of our families. When family members don't encourage us, support our dreams, and help us achieve our goals, our disappointment can affect our lives for years. That sadness is worse if family members are particularly neglectful or mean to us. We never forget what was said or what was done to us; we tend to carry that pain with us in a way that influences our relationships with other people. We often find it difficult to share our deepest thoughts and dreams for fear of being rejected or ridiculed. It is only through maturity that we come to a place where we can learn to love our family members and reject their destructive behaviors.

The Bible says that Joseph's father, Jacob (also called Israel), loved Joseph more than any of his brothers, not only because Jacob had loved Joseph's mother, Rachel, best of all his wives but also "because [Joseph] had been born to him in his old age" (Genesis 37:3). "When his brothers saw that their father loved [Joseph] more than any of them, they hated him and could not speak a kind word to him" (Genesis 37:4).

This is not a healthy pattern in a family. This kind of favoritism can disrupt relationships between brothers and sisters for their entire lives. It hurts to feel as if your parents pay more attention to your brother or sister than they do to you. After all, what is the matter with you? Aren't you worthy of being appreciated? Isn't there something equally special about you? Parents often make this choice of one child over the others. That choice sets in place a dynamic that can ruin relationships between not only siblings but also parents and children.

Joseph's brothers probably never told Joseph or their father how they felt about their mistreatment. Most likely, the family carried on with life as if everything was okay. Of course, it wasn't. Every day, even every happy moment, would have been tainted by the father's choice of Joseph as his favorite and the brothers' anger over this choice.

So often we carry the pain of rejection caused by family members because we are afraid to tell them what we feel and that their actions have hurt us. Holding on to such pain and anger makes for dishonest relationships. It keeps you from fulfilling your dreams. It interferes with your ability to have the deepest possible relationships with family members.

The situation in Joseph's family was made worse because Joseph wasn't just dad's favorite. He was also a dreamer. He dreamed about his future—and what he saw predicted a glorious future for him but a not-so-glorious future for his brothers. He saw them all bowing down at his feet (Genesis 37:5-8). When Joseph told his brothers about his dreams, they hated him for his ability to see a wonderful future. He dreamed again, and this time the glory for him included humility for his parents as well (Genesis 37:9). When he told his father about this dream, Jacob yelled at him and rejected his vision: "What's that supposed to mean? Are your mother and I and your brothers all going to come and bow down in front of you?" (Genesis 37:10 CEV).

One of the most painful things a young person can experience is to have his or her dreams rejected. You dream because you sense that you can do it. When I was a child, I was afraid to share my dreams with my mother and my uncles.

> **There will always be people who try to discourage you but keep dreaming anyway.**

They were likely to make jokes about me, laugh at me, or tell me I would never achieve my goals. My mother called me "good for nothing." Memories of my uncles' jokes and my mother's words stuck with me. As a result, I kept my dreams about my future as a doctor or basketball star to myself so that no one else would laugh at me.

You might have experienced the same thing. These negative tapes get burned into your brain. Here is my prescription: Keep dreaming anyway. There will always be people who try to discourage you. They might be family members, friends, or strangers. Your job is to believe in your image of yourself and who you can become. You can't allow other people to determine what you can become with God's help. You have to dream in spite of the doubters. When God shows you his plan for your future, you have to fight to keep that dream alive. The people who doubt you didn't create you, so don't let them define you.

Joseph's brothers were jealous that he was their father's favorite son. They resented his dream of becoming a community leader. So, it is probably correct to imagine that Joseph didn't hear many words of encouragement from his family. He heard only that he was being ridiculous to think that any of his dreams would ever come true.

One day Joseph's brothers decided they had had enough. The mere sight of Joseph made them angry. Because they were angry, they wanted to get rid of Joseph. The original plan was to kill him, but one of his brothers changed his mind, so they came up with a plan to sell Joseph into slavery. That's also hard to imagine. Some

> The people who doubt you didn't create you, so don't let them define you.

family members do this, though; they find you so intolerable that they send you away to a place where they will never see you again.

I've talked to teenagers and adults who don't have relationships with their brothers, sisters, or parents because of past pain and rejection. I was one of those people. My family didn't throw me away, though. I threw them away. The moment I had the chance to leave my family, I took it. My knowledge of my family story was complicated by lies. My parents were never married, and my father left when I was three. When I was eight, my mother told me that my father was killed in a car accident. I later learned that she told me this only because he was calling her trying to establish a relationship with me. She was so angry at him that she changed our phone number and told me that he was dead. Adults do crazy and selfish things all the time. You might have heard the statement that parents should love their children more than they hate each other. My mother forgot all about that.

When I was fourteen, I got a call from a ghost. My dad was alive and well. We managed to stay in touch for a year, and when I was fifteen I went to visit him in New Jersey. The experience was so different from anything I ever knew as a kid. He lived in a house (not an apartment) in the suburbs where there were no apparent drug dealers, crime, or gangs. I returned home to California after staying with him for the summer. Things were getting bad in my neighborhood. The gang activity had increased. The drug use and sales were up, and there were lots more murders. I made up my mind that I wanted to move away from that dangerous place and go to New Jersey to live with my father. My mother, uncles, grandparents, and friends didn't want me to go. My friends laughed at me and told me that I wasn't going anywhere and that I would always be stuck in the neighborhood. Because they never took my dream seriously, I had no problem leaving all of them—my mother, friends, and family members— behind. The people it hurt me to leave were my grandparents. But after telling my grandmother I wanted to go, she told me that I should. She believed in me, wanted me to have a better future, and loved me enough to let me go if that was what would save my life. For years, I never looked back.

If you never seek healing, you can never truly become whole.

I've met a lot of people who feel the same way about their families. They want to forget the painful experiences of growing up, so they never return to their childhood homes. They never heal those tattered relationships or tell the people they left behind how much they were hurt by the things that happened. But as I learned, if you never seek healing, you can never truly become whole.

While Joseph was living in slavery in Egypt he was sold into service in the household of an official named Potiphar.

When Potiphar saw that Joseph had favor with God, he put the younger man in charge of his home and property, entrusting Joseph with everything that he owned. Unfortunately, this great promotion didn't last long. Joseph caught the eye of Potiphar's wife, and when he refused to betray his boss by sleeping with her, she accused him of assaulting her and got him thrown in jail (Genesis 39:1-20).

Even in prison, God was with Joseph. The prison warden recognized that Joseph had leadership qualities, and so he promoted Joseph to care for the other prisoners (Genesis 39:21-23). And Joseph's experience as a dreamer allowed him to become an interpreter of other people's dreams—first of his fellow prisoners and eventually of Pharaoh, the ruler of Egypt. By interpreting the dreams of others, Joseph saw his own dreams come true. He became savior of the nation in a time of crisis, and he was promoted anew, to become second-in-command to Pharaoh with all of Egypt at his feet.

Even when it seems that life is not going your way, God will allow some people to see your talents and to open doors for you. Slavery is a terrible condition. Prison may have been even worse! But Joseph was able to work his way out of those situations in ways that were not usually available to others in similar straits.

Over time Joseph married the daughter of a prominent Egyptian priest, and they had two sons. Joseph named the firstborn Manasseh, "because God has made me forget all my trouble and all my father's household" (Genesis 41:51). Joseph named his second son Ephraim, stating, "It is because God has made me fruitful in the land of my suffering" (Genesis 41:52).

Joseph had moved on with his life and thought the pain of his past was behind him. He had come to peace with not having a relationship with his birth family and had built a new life. But God, as you have learned in previous chapters, is about reconciliation and healing. The dream that God showed Joseph was becoming a reality. Joseph was growing and advancing as a leader. But Joseph's dream included his family, so the issues of his past were not over yet.

When we have been hurt by family members, we tend to want to ignore these relationship issues. We may feel that these relationships are holding us back. But the reality is that we are born into our families for a reason. At times it may feel like our loved ones are the source of much of our pain, but that is not God's plan. Our families are meant to be a source of strength, support, encouragement, and love. They are a source of pain when there is no honesty, communication, or willingness to think about the well-being of someone other than ourselves. And some families are so tragically wounded that you may have to find a way to heal without them. But you must first try all avenues that are not dangerous to you, physically and spiritually.

Joseph didn't know it, but God had put him on a journey that led him toward healing the wounds in his family.[1] Do you remember I said that while serving Potiphar, Joseph was accused of a crime he didn't commit and was thrown in jail? Once again, just as he had with his brothers, Joseph experienced punishment and dealt with difficulties not because of anything that he did but because of other people who wanted to do harm to him.

As a teenager I knew a lot of people who did jail time. Lots

of kids sold drugs, were involved with gangs, committed rob-
beries, and engaged in all kinds of illegal behaviors to get
money, hoping that they would one day have enough to get
out of poverty or to just have the same nice things that other
people had. This is the kind of future planning that happens
in poor neighborhoods. It doesn't work well. It's what happens when people don't have positive dreams and have no
one to believe in their ability to do well.

I believe to this day that a lot of the things my friends and
I did had nothing to do with gaining access to easy money.
Many of them had to do with problems in our families that
caused us not to value and respect other people as much as
we should have. There were times when we would get together and talk about what was going on in our lives, our
dreams for the future, and the challenges we were dealing
with at home. We discussed the anger we felt because we did
not feel that our dreams would ever be realized.

When you feel that people don't value or care about you,
when you don't hear words of encouragement on a consis-
tent basis, and when you feel controlled by your circumstances, you become angry and defensive. The result is that
you don't value other people because you don't value yourself. You don't have much power because you have given it
away. Even if you don't know it, there are people who love
you and who believe that you can do great things. They see
the reflection of God's image in you. They know that it is
never too late for you to start over. The toughest fight in life
is the fight to keep believing in yourself. The power to control
your actions, claim your future, and fulfill your dreams is in
your hands. And you are in God's hands.

> There are people who see the reflection of God's image in you, people who believe you can do great things.

There are people who see the reflection of God's image in you, people who believe you can do great things.

Joseph ran into a lot of challenges in life, but God was still in control of his future. Recall that while Joseph was still in jail, Pharaoh began to have troubled dreams. Pharaoh sent for every wise man and magician in the land, but no one could interpret his dreams. A member of Pharaoh's staff (a former prisoner himself) reported that another prisoner, Joseph, had the gift of interpreting dreams. When Pharaoh's nightmares continued, he was so desperate to sleep that Joseph was asked to interpret Pharaoh's dreams. His interpretation was provided in a clever way. As a result, Pharaoh put Joseph in charge of the entire palace and all of the people in Egypt (Genesis 41:1-40).

Joseph's life was back on track. He began to see the results of everything God had shown him in his early dreams. But something still needed to happen to make his life whole. Joseph needed to talk to his family. When the famine came (much like what we experienced during the Great Recession, when there was a lot of unemployment and little money for food and rent), Joseph's father, Jacob, sent his ten oldest sons to Egypt to buy food. Anyone who wanted to buy food in Egypt had to go to Joseph first. When Joseph's older brothers got to Egypt, it had been so long since they had seen him that they didn't even recognize their brother. They never would have guessed that their brother would be ruler of Egypt under Pharaoh. After all, they thought that their brother was still living as a slave after all these years. He recognized them, though. Things were happening just the way Joseph had imagined. He was a leader of his community. He was in a position to help his family.

Joseph thought he had moved on and let go of his family issues until his brothers arrived in Egypt. All of his pain and feelings of rejection flooded back. He remembered how much his brothers hated him and discouraged his dreams. Joseph's old pain caused him to use his power as a leader to speak harshly to his brothers and to make them afraid of him. Sometimes the pain we experience growing up can distort our dreams. Then our good sense gets clouded by our egos. We take our pain and anger and throw it in the faces of the people who hurt us.

You will find that it is a useless exercise to try to get back at people who hurt you. I used to spend time thinking about how I would get back at the people who hurt me. I would say to myself, "If they ever ask me for money I'm going to say no, even if I have it to give." I would think about how I would respond if members of my family tried to contact me. I had decided that I would not answer the phone if they called. In short, I was planning to make them feel as bad as they had made me feel. I was going to reject them the same way they rejected me. I wanted to make them feel lonely and helpless because they made me feel lonely and helpless. I made the mistake of thinking that revenge would bring about healing. But the truth is that it only creates more pain. Honestly, even spending time thinking about revenge causes you pain. You can't think about and plan negative behavior and expect positive outcomes! Negative thoughts and actions lead to negative feelings and outcomes. End of story.

Revenge does not heal. Love does.

Joseph realized that he was angry because he was still hurting. He was still hurting because he cared for his brothers. The truth is that you can't have sad feelings about people unless there is love behind it. Instead of rejecting his feelings, Joseph accepted the fact that he still

> **Revenge does not heal. Love does.**

loved and missed his brothers and the rest of his family. And if we are honest, the only reason we get angry with people in our family is because we care about them. If we didn't care, there would be no reason to be angry with them.

Joseph accepted that his anger was worth working through because he did care, he missed his brothers, and it hurt him to see them hurting. The time came when Joseph decided to be courageous enough to let his brothers know who he was, share his feelings of hurt, and let them know that he loved and cared about them. Joseph forgave his brothers for selling him into slavery in Egypt. That is a *lot* of forgiveness (Genesis 45:4-8).

Young men and women have a hard time admitting their feelings. In many families, we as young men are taught not to cry, show emotions, or talk about how we feel. We are told to be tough and manly. Though it is changing a bit, everything we learn teaches us not to be so sensitive, not to "act like girls." Given what society teaches us about keeping our feelings in, it is not surprising that boys, young men, and men don't do well sharing our inner selves. Hiding feelings doesn't take any courage; it only shows that you're afraid to be honest with yourself and with others.

God wants you to be courageous enough to express yourself so that you can fight for what you want.

If Joseph had bottled up his true feelings and shown only rage and anger toward his brothers, they would not have received the healing and forgiveness they wanted. As was the case with Joseph, God wants you to be courageous enough to express yourself so that you can fight for what you want. God seeks healing for you and your family. All of us want better relationships with our parents, brothers, and sisters. We want to be able to tell them how we feel and have them support us in return. If that's what you want, then be like Joseph and fight for it. You deserve healthy relationships, and God wants you to have them.

Beginning: Joseph was rejected by his brothers, had problems with his father, and was thrown in jail for a crime he didn't commit.

Ending: Joseph was a leader who saved his family and community during a famine.

What made the difference: Joseph never gave up on his dream, and God never gave up on Joseph. Even though his brothers rejected him and he had problems with his dad, Joseph still loved his family and found it in his heart to forgive them.

What Now?

The following are activities that can be completed and questions that can be answered in Christian education classes or Bible study or written as answers in a journal that records your spiritual journey.

1. God is about restoring relationships, not throwing people away. Sometimes things that happened in our families make us never want to speak to certain people again. Who are the people in your family that you feel this way about?
   a. What did they do to hurt you?
   b. Did you do anything to hurt them?
   c. How can you forgive them?
   d. If you hurt them, are you willing to ask for forgiveness?
2. What is your healthiest family relationship?
   a. What makes it healthy?
   b. How will you keep it healthy?
3. What is your unhealthiest family relationship?
   a. What makes it unhealthy?
   b. How long has it been this unhealthy?
   c. How will you make it more healthy?

Get Prayed Up

God, even though my family has hurt me, I still love them. I need your help to overcome the pain: the pain of feeling rejected and the pain of feeling alone. I know that I have disappointed you at times. I let my anger with past pain get the best of me, but, God, I'm coming to you to say I'm sorry. I accept your forgiveness, and I am ready to move in a new direction—a new direction that frees me from the pain and mistakes of the past. God, I know that you love me and that I am not a mistake. Teach me how to accept your love and to love with purpose. Set me free from anger, guilt, doubt, and shame. I thank you, God, for what you're doing in my life. Thank you for new opportunities and a fresh start. From this day forward I will do the best that I can to live free from anger and the pain of my past. With your guidance and your strength I know that I will be successful. Thank you, God, for always being there for me, hearing my cry, and removing my sorrow. I know that I can count on you to help me achieve my dreams. Amen.

Notes

1. In most cases, it is advisable to heal wounds between family members. Sometimes this can be done with the family members alone, and sometimes professional help is needed. In some cases, the damage to family members is so terrible that it is advisable to walk away; however, this decision should be made with professional help.

8

The Boy with an Evil Spirit

Breaking Unhealthy Cycles

Ending: The father took his son to see Jesus and overcame his unbelief.

Beginning: The boy was possessed by evil spirits. The father had no belief that his son would improve.

"What are you arguing with them about?" he asked. A man in the crowd answered, "Teacher, I brought you my son, who is possessed by a spirit that has robbed him of speech. Whenever it seizes him, it throws him to the ground. He foams at the mouth, gnashes his teeth and becomes rigid. I asked your disciples to drive out the spirit, but they could not." (Mark 9:16-18)

This Scripture describes an episode about a boy possessed by something that his community did not understand. This terrible *something* tossed the boy around; it was interpreted as an evil spirit. Even though no medical explanations were given for the condition of the boy, in today's medical system these symptoms might well have been diagnosed as epilepsy. Jesus had not named the boy's spiritual possession. Instead, his concern was that the father doubted that the son's internal demons could be healed: "Jesus asked the boy's father, 'How long has he been like this?' 'From childhood,' he answered. 'It has often thrown him into fire or water to kill him. But if you can do anything, take pity on us and help us.' '"If you can?"' said Jesus. 'Everything is possible for him who believes'" (Mark 9:21-23).

I'm not so sure the father didn't believe, but he did have doubts. He brought his son to the disciples because of what he heard Jesus had done for others. He dared to hope, to believe that healing was possible—but that faith and hope were mixed with doubt. His son had had this problem for a long time, and nothing the father had tried in the past had helped the boy. Naturally, the father had doubts, but he wouldn't have taken his son to the disciples if he hadn't believed there was a chance they could help the boy.

So, how does doubt happen? Doubt happens because we see frightening behaviors that repeat and get worse. As a result, we begin to feel that the behavior will never change and nothing can be done about it. The boy's father was certain that his son's gyrations, foaming at the mouth, and other demonic and dangerous behaviors made it impossible to keep his son safe. As a result, the father had doubts that he could do anything to help his son and wasn't so sure God could, either. This was the state the father was in when he met Jesus. This important meeting reminded the father that he had been so overwhelmed by his son's possession by an evil spirit that he had lost sight of the power of God. And so the father said, "I do believe; help me overcome my unbelief!" (Mark 9:24).

When I read this story of a father trying to find a way to help his son to stop hurting himself, it reminds me of my mother's addiction. When I'm talking to young people across the country I hear a lot of stories like mine. It's a complete role reversal of what we see in this biblical story. A lot of young people have a parent who does things to harm himself or herself. In many homes today it's the son or daughter who is looking for someone who can help the parent.

You may have someone close to you who is possessed by a modern-day version of evil spirits. Some may be involved with liquid spirits that bring out their demons; alcoholism is a terrible beast. Other friends and family members are addicted to a wide range of legal and illegal drugs. Drug and alcohol addictions stem from the need to medicate unhealed wounds. Addicted persons, we now know, are hurting themselves by fighting a demon that can only destroy them, their healthy relationships with family members, their jobs, and themselves.

In much the same way that this father's son changed from normal to possessed, so a variety of demons can turn our parents or other loved ones into people we don't recognize. Demons take many forms—in biblical times, conditions such as epilepsy and schizophrenia were likely attributed to demonic possession. Today, addiction is probably one of the most damaging demons in the lives of families and youth.

Understanding Why

In the Bible passage, you will notice that the father never asked Jesus why his son was hurting himself. The father only asked if Jesus could heal his son. In fact, when the evil spirit seized the son and spoke to the father in front of Jesus, Jesus did not ask the father how this happened, nor did he blame him for his son's behavior. Instead, Jesus asked, "How long has he been like this?" "From childhood," the father answered (Mark 9:21).

Sometimes we spend time trying to understand why our parent is hurting himself or herself. The truth is that we won't always be able to understand why or how our parent falls into addiction. Sometimes the reasons are buried beneath so much pain that our moms and dads can't explain their feelings or describe the source of the problems. But as their children, our job is not to figure out why. Our job is to never give up on our parents, to love them and believe that things can get better if they (and we) get the right help.

> Our job is to never give up on our parents, to love them and believe that things can get better if they (and we) get the right help.

We have discussed the ways that people in pain turn their feelings outward so that their families, friends, and community members feel the impact. What we hear less often is that hurt people might also hurt themselves. They may medicate their pain away through the abuse of alcohol and other drugs.[1] They may become depressed.[2] You know what it feels like to be hurt, to feel as if your parents don't understand that what they are doing to themselves is hurting you because you love them and care about their health.

It is when people cannot find peace with their pain that they hurt themselves through drugs and alcohol. But here is what is important to know: Just as Jesus made himself available to the father whose son was demon-possessed, so he will make himself available to a parent or someone else you love who is struggling with personal demons.

Stop the Blame Game

The man had heard that Jesus was conducting miracles of healing for people who came to him with their pains and problems. This father was specifically concerned that his son was in pain, hurting himself, and no one could help (Mark 9:16-18). The son wasn't accepted by the community. This boy demonstrated strange behaviors. The father felt encouraged that something good might happen if the son could just get to Jesus.

The father arrived at the place where Jesus was healing people. The disciples were also reported to have healing powers. When the man brought his son to the disciples and requested a healing, the disciples thought that they were not up to the challenge of curing this boy. An argument started. "When they came to the other disciples, they saw a large crowd around them and the teachers of the law arguing with them" (Mark 9:14). After such a long journey to relieve his son's suffering, I'm sure that the boy's father was angry. His son needed help. Why could other people be healed and not his son? Did these disciples have the power to heal, or were they trying to pull off a scam in Jesus' name? The disciples were unlikely to have had easy answers to these questions. It is possible that the disciples had their own concerns about the father's efforts for his son. Why had the father waited so long to get help for his son?

The Bible doesn't tell us what was said during the argument, and it doesn't much matter. What was important was that the boy needed help and healing. Arguments turn into pointless circles of blaming the other person, and nothing gets done that solves the problem. Blaming makes everyone defensive. When we want someone to become whole again, the first thing we have to do is stop trying to assign blame for what's wrong. In your family you may hear other family members talking about what led to your mother's or father's addiction. They may say things such as, "Your mom brought it on herself because of her own choices," or, "It's because of how your father was mistreated by his parents." The bottom line is that it doesn't matter who or what caused the addiction. Blaming doesn't solve the problem or get people the help they need.

> When we want someone to become whole again, the first thing we have to do is stop trying to assign blame for what's wrong.

The Church and the Power of Change

"I asked your disciples to drive out the spirit, but they could not." "O unbelieving generation," Jesus replied, "how long shall I stay with you? How long shall I put up with you? Bring the boy to me." (Mark 9:18-19 NIV)

Addiction is a selfish behavior. When my mother became addicted to drugs and alcohol, she became an absentee parent who lived in the same house as I did. Does that sound familiar? Maybe your father lives in the same house with you, but you never get to spend time with him because he's sleeping off last night's party—or at a new one by the time you get home. Maybe your mom is never around to talk to or attend the big events in your life, because she's working multiple jobs to pay for her addiction. In those circumstances, you feel like your mother or father is an absentee parent. "Present absence" can be more harmful than not being there at all.

As I've told you, my mother was addicted to drugs and alcohol for most of my childhood. Living with an addict was an unstable and unsafe life. My mother's drug use made her disappear from the family home for weeks at a time. After I moved to live with my father in New Jersey, I would call to speak to her—but my relatives usually did not know where she was. To protect my feelings, they tended to tell me that my mother had left the house just before I called. After a while I gave up on trying to speak to her. I was angry with her for being a drug addict, for abandoning me, for behavior that hurt both of us. Still, I loved her. For more than eight years my mother and I talked only two or three times a year, but that was if she happened to be home when I called or if she called me to ask for money.

Earlier, I mentioned a letter that I received from my mother. Initially, I was afraid to open it, but when I finally opened the envelope, I saw that my mother had put lots of work into the letter. It was a long letter, several pages stapled together. Here's part of my mother's letter:

> Hi Romal,
> I haven't talked to you in a long time but I hear that you have been doing well. I didn't call because I feel like you're mad at me. I have my own apartment. I'm living in Vallejo not far from mom's house. I'm not running the streets any more. I got a job working with elderly people in hospice care. I'm studying to become a nurse. I stay with my patients sometimes to keep them company, help around the house, cook lunch and dinner for them. I joined church and I'm getting baptized next week. I haven't been drinking or anything like that for a while. The church has really been helpful to me and the people are really nice. My friends there are really supportive. We spend a lot of time together and they also have a recovery program that I am in.

My mother's letter made me cry. Her story was similar to that of the boy whose father brought him to be healed by Jesus. Both my mother and that boy had been possessed by evil spirits. These spirits deeply troubled them, and when someone we care about is hurting himself or herself, it hurts the entire family. If the behavior is bad enough, it can also hurt people in the community.

If you look at my mother's letter, you'll see that the church did not heal my mother. The church was supportive of her and encouraged her journey to wholeness. Church is a place where believers worship together. Many churches also provide supportive ministries for people with specific needs. But church alone cannot heal anyone.

Here is what is important to understand: What truly changed my mother was the love and presence of God. God does not live *only* in church. God lives in the world and in each one of us. My mother found a reason to love herself again because she knew that God loved her for who she was and for who she was becoming. God loved her in spite of her mistakes because God was more concerned with her future than with her past. God showed my mother what unconditional love looked and felt like by surrounding her with nonjudgmental people who treated her with respect and dignity and helped her learn to love herself. That's what led my mother to seek treatment in a drug rehabilitation program, to participate in counseling, and to find a job that allowed her to work with hospice patients who needed the kind of loving support that she had the heart and the experience to provide.

My mother's journey to recovery and wholeness wasn't easy. It isn't easy for anyone to overcome an addiction. But it is amazing what happens when demons leave our spirits. I gained the mother I had always wanted. When my mother died, I was angry for a long time, not with her but with God. I was angry because, after all of those years of watching her hurt herself with drugs and alcohol, we were finally getting the chance to build a relationship when she was free from addiction. Our relationship was amazing. I would send for her to visit her grandchildren and me; she would buy them gifts and play with them. We were finally a family. For about four years we had a great relationship. But then my mother was diagnosed with lung cancer. When I found out, I begged her to come and live with me. I had just bought a bigger house, so there was plenty of room. She had finally agreed, but before we had a chance to move her into the new home, she got seriously ill. The doctor said it was pneumonia. I knew it was time to get her and bring her to my home in Maryland so that I could care for her. I arrived on a Tuesday. We spent the day together, and she died the next morning—just two months after she had confided that she had cancer. I never got to bring her to DC; she never got to see her new home.

I had always dreamed of rescuing my mother from the hood, and just when I was about to get my chance, she died. I was angry with God and angry with myself. I didn't want anything to do with church, preaching, or ministry. I wanted to punish God and myself. But I later realized that it was not God's fault, nor was it God's plan for her to get cancer. The truth is, God gave us a blessing. The blessing was restoring our relationship before she died and granting her time to get to know her grandchildren and the opportunity to know that I was okay. Most of all, the blessing was knowing that before she died, my mother had a relationship with God.

The Road to Recovery

"Bring the boy to me." So they brought him. . . .
Jesus asked the boy's father, "How long has he been
like this?" "From childhood," he answered. "It has
often thrown him into fire or water to kill him."
(Mark 9:19,21-22)

Cycles of pain, mental illness, self-destruction, addiction,
and other personal demons take years to form. When Jesus
asked, "How long has he been like this?" the boy's father
replied, "From childhood." Pain and personal demons happen to children, teenagers, young adults, and seniors. When
parents engage in self-destructive behavior, their children
don't understand why the behaviors developed or how they
can help get rid of them.

The road to recovery from any form of disease or pain can
be long. It's a process of letting go of the addiction and letting
go of the cause or causes, learning to heal from past experiences, learning to love yourself, and accepting the love that
God has for you. Life had to be difficult for the boy in this
story. He had to live with how poorly other people thought
of him. He may have felt shame because he was different,
and grief because of all the opportunities for fun and friend-
ship that he missed as a child. He may also have felt that he
let his father down. This boy had a lot on his mind. We know
for sure, though, that his father never gave up on him. He
was doing what committed parents do. This father was looking under every rock and in every cranny for the miracle that
would heal his child.

Don't Be Defeated by Doubt

"But if you can do anything, take pity on us and help
us." . . . "Everything is possible for one who believes." . . . "I do believe, but help me overcome my
unbelief." (Mark 9:22-24)

Some people will tell you that you should not doubt God.
I say, Why not? We are human and we each have doubts
about many things in life. Doubt is natural. The good thing
is that God is not like us. God does not judge us for being
honest about our feelings. Our Creator is God enough to
handle our doubts and help us overcome them. The father in
this story had doubts. He had been trying for years to find
answers to what was wrong with his son, and no one knew.
For years he watched his son suffer, and all he could do was
watch it happen. He had no luck with Jesus' disciples or doc-
tors of medicine. The father's doubts were the result of his
experiences with people, not with God.

It is important to know the difference between doubting
the people whom God created and doubting God. Understanding this difference helps us when we try to make disciples of other people. Rather than asking, "How will I get this
person to church?" the real question is, "How will I get this
person to Jesus?"

In the Bible passage that we have been studying, the boy's
father doubts that his son can be healed. He may have begun
to disbelieve that anyone was able help his son. The father
was honest enough to admit his doubts to Jesus and to ask
Jesus directly for help. He was able to do this even though he

had often been disappointed and experienced failure in his efforts to find healing for his son.

As is the case with this father, most of our doubts come from failed personal efforts or when we relied on other people and they failed us. We may doubt ourselves, those relationships, and God. The good news is that God can take it. God always has our backs. The more we experience success when we trust God, the more our doubts about God will begin to fade.

The road to letting go of doubt about God is not easy, though. It requires one thing that everyone hates to be—obedient. Obedient to God. Obedience is doing what God wants you to do, trusting that God has your best interests in mind, and believing that in the end God will make sure you are okay. Though it can sometimes be difficult for you to understand, God's plan is always better. Why? Because God created you, and God knows what you were destined to do with your life.

When my mother decided to become obedient to God, she had been addicted to drugs and alcohol for almost fifteen years. She had doubts about whether or not she could get clean from drugs on her own. What helped her kick her addiction and stay committed to the process of wholeness? My mother found that while she often doubted herself, she never doubted God. She would pray, "God, I'm not sure that I can do it, but I know that you can. I know that I am weak, but you can give me the strength to beat this. That's what you want for me. I need you, Lord. And I need you to send people into my life who want the same thing for me that you want for me."

In order for you to overcome your doubts, such as whether God can heal someone you love from drug or alcohol abuse, if you are smart enough to achieve your dreams, if life will ever get better, you have to ask yourself: "What is the source of my doubt?" Then you must be honest with yourself about the answer and confess it to God. Here's an example of what it might look like:

> God, I have doubts about _____, and this is why. My experiences have sometimes hurt me deeply. But I understand that I cannot use that hurt as an excuse for not claiming the wonderful life that you have made available to me. I know, God, that you can't fail and that you won't fail me. I will try harder to experience my blessings and need your help to do that. Once I am paying better attention to your goodness to me, my doubts will stop.

That's what the father meant when he said to Jesus, "I do believe; help me overcome my unbelief!" (Mark 9:24).

Ask God to help you overcome your disbelief, and get ready for God to something amazing!

When did the father's doubts about God disappear? The moment when Jesus healed his son was the moment when he overcame his disbelief. Once he knew that his son would not suffer anymore, he never again doubted the power of God. The same is true for you. Ask God to help you overcome your disbelief, and get ready for God to do something amazing!

Let God Use You to Show People What Jesus Can Do

> When Jesus saw that a crowd was running to the scene, he rebuked the evil spirit. "You deaf and mute spirit," he said, "I command you, come out of him and never enter him again." The spirit shrieked, convulsed him violently and came out. (Mark 9:25-26)

Everyone in the community knew about the man's son and his condition. They also knew that the father had brought his son to Jesus. Of course we know the question that was on their minds: Could Jesus heal this boy after all these years of having an evil spirit come on him and cause him to hurt himself? People were curious to see if the boy could be healed; they ran to watch and listen to the man's conversation with Jesus. They clearly heard the message that doubt will not get in the way of God's blessings.

The topic of healing is not one that many people want to address publicly. It can be embarrassing. It may be surprising to learn that asking God to heal you is nothing to be ashamed of. It's something to celebrate and be proud of. Having the confidence to trust God with your life, heart, feelings, and soul is not an easy task. Overcoming doubts can be almost impossible. But understand this: You are not a hero who has saved yourself by yourself. You have to put your life in God's hands.

There is no shame in wanting, seeking, and receiving healing from God. The father in this story had nothing to lose and everything to gain by taking his son to Jesus. If Jesus was not a healer, his son would remain in his present state. The father and family were used to dealing with that. But if Jesus could help, even a little bit, that would be a blessing. Having learned that healing was possible, this father now was part of the community of those who could state that "anything is possible for him who believes!"

Steps to Break the Cycle

The following steps can be useful to you or a loved one you wish to help.

1. Accept that you alone cannot help the person to overcome addiction.

2. Don't let people get you caught up in a blame game, because blaming people doesn't solve the problem or help the person in need of healing.

3. Never give up on people you love when they are hurting themselves, because that's when they need your love the most.

4. Look for help.

5. Remember it's okay to have doubts about the person overcoming addiction, but don't let the doubts stop you from trying.

6. Admit when you have doubts about God and God's ability to help you.

7. Be proud of your accomplishments, what God has done for you, and the person you are trying to help.

Be Prepared for Resistance

"You deaf and mute spirit, . . . I command you, come out of him and never enter him again." The spirit

shrieked, convulsed him violently and came out.
(Mark 9:25)

Helping someone overcome addiction is not easy. It requires lots of work for the person who is in pain and the person or people supporting him or her.

Whenever there is resistance to overcoming addiction, the addicted person does not have control. It's the spirit of that person's pain (illness, trauma, addiction) trying to maintain control over his or her life. Remember that the person is fighting the addiction, not you. Even in the process of trying to get better, that person may yell at you and be mean, but it's not your fault and it's not really aimed at you. He or she is struggling, and sometimes fighting to overcome addiction makes people lash out.

For example, the evil spirit showed great resistance to allowing the healing of the boy. "The spirit shrieked, convulsed him violently and came out." My mother's healing was also a difficult process; alcohol and drug addictions change the minds, bodies, and spirits of the addicted person. Getting well isn't easy, and there were many times that I thought that my mother wasn't going to make it. She craved drugs even though she was not getting high. She would get angry for no reason at all.

Your mother, father, or any other person you love who is trying to overcome an addition needs someone else to turn to for help when she or he is working to heal. That person is you and any other person you can find who loves your parent as much as you do. My mother needed support, love, and encouragement. Healing from her addiction was hard.

That's the same thing you will have to give the person in your life. To support her, she spent time in the substance abuse program at her church learning how to fight the addiction so that she could truly be healed. She put together a support group, people who could remind her that she was loved, talented, smart, beautiful, and capable of beating her addiction. She needed to keep believing in herself and having faith in God. We reminded her that she would face resistance in the forms of anger and rejection. Addiction has many voices. By working together, praying together, and supporting my mother as she worked through drug treatment, she recovered from a lifetime of demons. God broke her cycle of pain. That's what it takes, and these are the kinds of things you and others who try to help someone heal will have to give that person to beat the addiction.

Jesus did the same for the young boy. Once the boy was healed, the disciples asked a question that many people ask in their own circumstances: "Why couldn't we drive it out?" We often feel like failures when we cannot provide help for severe problems. Perhaps our roles are to be different. Support is an important kind of help; we don't have to solve the problem.

What we can do is to begin to dream of a better future. We can dream of what life will be like for ourselves if we or a friend or family member has been plagued by evil spirits. I used to dream about what it would be like for my mother and me. When it finally happened, God exceeded my expectations. I learned that my imagination was far too limited to understand what God had in store for my mother's healing and for our restored relationship. God can do the same thing for the person in your life who overcomes addiction. Your relationship with your mother, father, or another person in your family will be amazing when she or he heals.

Prayer is having a conversation with God. When people are hurting themselves, they don't have the power to change, and you don't have the power to change them. That means you have to rely on a power that is greater than yourself. That power is God.

I've since learned that when you dream about the change that you want in your life or the life of a loved one, you must talk to God about it in prayer. If you keep your heart and mind open to the possibility of healing, God's healing will come.

> "But I will restore you to health
> and heal your wounds,"
> declares the LORD,
> "because you are called an outcast,
> Zion for whom no one cares."
> —Jeremiah 30:17

My mother broke my heart many times during the years of her addiction and recovery. I finally realized that there was nothing I could do to change her. Eventually, I had no other choice but to ask God to protect and heal my mother, whose addiction took her to dangerous places. It took years for God to answer my prayers, but God was faithful. But I never stopped praying or believing that my mother would be healed or imagining a healthy relationship with my mother once her addiction was over. My point to you is, never give up on the people you love. Believe they can get better. Pray for them, and ask God what role you may have to play to bring the person whom you care about to wholeness. Trust me, it can happen. I've seen it for myself.

Beginning: The boy was possessed by evil spirits. The father had no belief that his son would improve.
Ending: The father took his son to see Jesus and overcame his unbelief.
What made the difference: The father never gave up on trying to find help. The father asked God to help him overcome his unbelief. The father did what was in his power to do and let God do what was in God's power to do. In the end the father's attitude led him to Jesus, and Jesus was able to heal his son.

What Now?

The following are some things that you can do to help you overcome the pain of anger and doubt. You can write your answers in this book or in a journal that records your spiritual journey.

1. If you have ever known someone who has been addicted to demons of drugs or alcohol, please describe what you learned from his or her behavior (possession). In what way did healing take place for that person (if it did)? Be specific.
2. From what issue or personal pain do you require God's healing? Be specific. As an example, you might state, "I cannot forgive my aunt for a comment that she made about my father's or my mother's addiction. I need to empty my heart

of this anger so that I can be free to accept your blessings and love."

3. If someone you love is hurting himself or herself because of the demons associated with drugs or alcohol abuse, are there people who love and care about that person as much as you do? How can these people help?

4. Like the boy's father, sometimes we have doubts about anyone being able to help the person we love get better and stop hurting himself or herself. In order to stay focused and determined to help someone in your family overcome demons, you have to overcome your doubts. Write down your doubts and the cause for the doubts. Find ways to overcome them.

Example: I had doubts about my mother getting better because it seemed that every time she tried to defeat her demons of drug abuse, she would fail. I doubted things would change because I saw her fail in the past. I overcame my doubt by continuing to love her and by trusting that God would find a way to heal her. I also found people to talk to who would encourage me and encourage her. We each developed our own support groups.

My doubt: She would never get better.

Cause of my doubt: Her past attempts and failures to overcome demons of addiction.

How I overcome doubt: Asking other people to support me in trying to help her; developing a support group for my mother and also one for myself.

Get Prayed Up

God, I have dreamed that when _____
is healed and our relationship is better, we will be able to
_____. But, God, I
know that my imagination is limited and that you can do
more than anything I could ever think of on my own. So,
God, I want what you want, and I want it when you want it.
Give me the strength to wait patiently and the courage to love
_____ even when
_____ hurts himself or herself
through the addiction. Teach me to love _____
until change comes. When it happens, I will give you the
praise, glory, and honor because you are the source of all
good things.

Notes
1. "Self-Medication of Anxiety Symptoms with Drugs or
Alcohol Associated with Increased Risk of Developing Substance Use Disorders," *Science Daily* (August 1, 2011),
http://www.sciencedaily.com/releases/2011/08/1108117
2550.htm (accessed March 11, 2013).
2. Among the resources available from the National Association on Mental Illness (NAMI) are the "Family Guide to
Adolescent Depression" (2009) and "What Families Need
to Know about Adolescent Depression" (2011). Search on-
line at http://www.nami.org.

You're Already Good Enough

It's Your Turn to Win

After reading these stories of how young people in the Bible overcame the challenges in their lives, families, and communities, you've probably experienced all kinds of emotions and have a million thoughts running through your head. Don't be afraid to let yourself be emotional. It's okay to be afraid, scared, nervous, and sad. The key is learning the cause of what you are feeling, being honest about your feelings, and finding a way to turn what you feel into positive actions that keep you on the right track for living the life that God wants you to live, the life that you dream about and want for yourself. You are already good enough to achieve your dreams. You have what it takes to make your life better.

As I wrote this book, there were times when I felt sad, angry, overwhelmed, afraid, and even excited about what God has done in my life. And I want you to know that not only *can* God do it for you, but also God *is going* to do it for you. How is it going to happen? It will happen the same way it does for the people in the stories you just read. Like them, you have to believe in your dreams, overcome your fears, determine what you want, not blame yourself for the mistakes of others, and trust God to help you through every situation in your life.

The main thing I want you to know about everything that you have read in these stories and my story is that you can overcome any situations in your life. I hope they are an example to you that no matter where you are now, it doesn't have to determine your future. *God's Graffiti* is "tagged" on the lives of people all around you. You need to learn to recognize it in your own life as well. God has an amazing future in store for you. The challenges you face are not meant for you to give up. God didn't cause them, but God can help you overcome them—and then God will use them to bring about your destiny, as he did in the story of Joseph and others.

Remember what I said about graffiti at the beginning of the book: People don't always understand it. To some people it looks like a bunch of colors, confusion, and images that are hard to understand. That's how our lives can be when we look at what we go through. At first it seems messy and confusing, but in the end you learn that it is something beautiful. Just like any other kind of art, it's not meant for everyone to get it. But the artist knows what he or she is doing and the story he or she is trying to tell. God has a plan and a purpose in mind for your life. In the end it all makes sense. When the artwork of your life is finished, you will be able to look at it and see it as something that is amazing. You will be able to look back and see that God was with you in every situation, how God brought you out of it, and then how God used it to make you stronger on the journey to the place that God has for you.

Just like the young men and women in the Bible, you are an amazing person. You're amazing because God created you to be amazing. You are talented, smart, beautiful, handsome, courageous, strong, and destined to do great things. Why? Because God made you that way. God doesn't make mistakes; God makes miracles. My story and the stories you just read are proof.

Some people thought I was crazy to write a book that tells so much about my life and my family. But I did it because I wanted God to use what I have been through to help other young people like me. I did it because I didn't care what other people might think. I believe that if telling my story will help other young people see that they can overcome the challenges and the pain to do great things, then that's all that matters to me.

Believe in yourself. Believe that God is with you. Ask people to help you. Do whatever it takes to be the great person you were created to be and achieve the things that God wants you to achieve. You are God's graffiti. You're God's work of art. And no matter what you go through or what anyone else says, I want you to know and God wants you to know that you are already good enough to do great things.